ONE HUNDRED AND FIFTY
YEARS OF MUSIC PUBLISHING
IN THE UNITED STATES

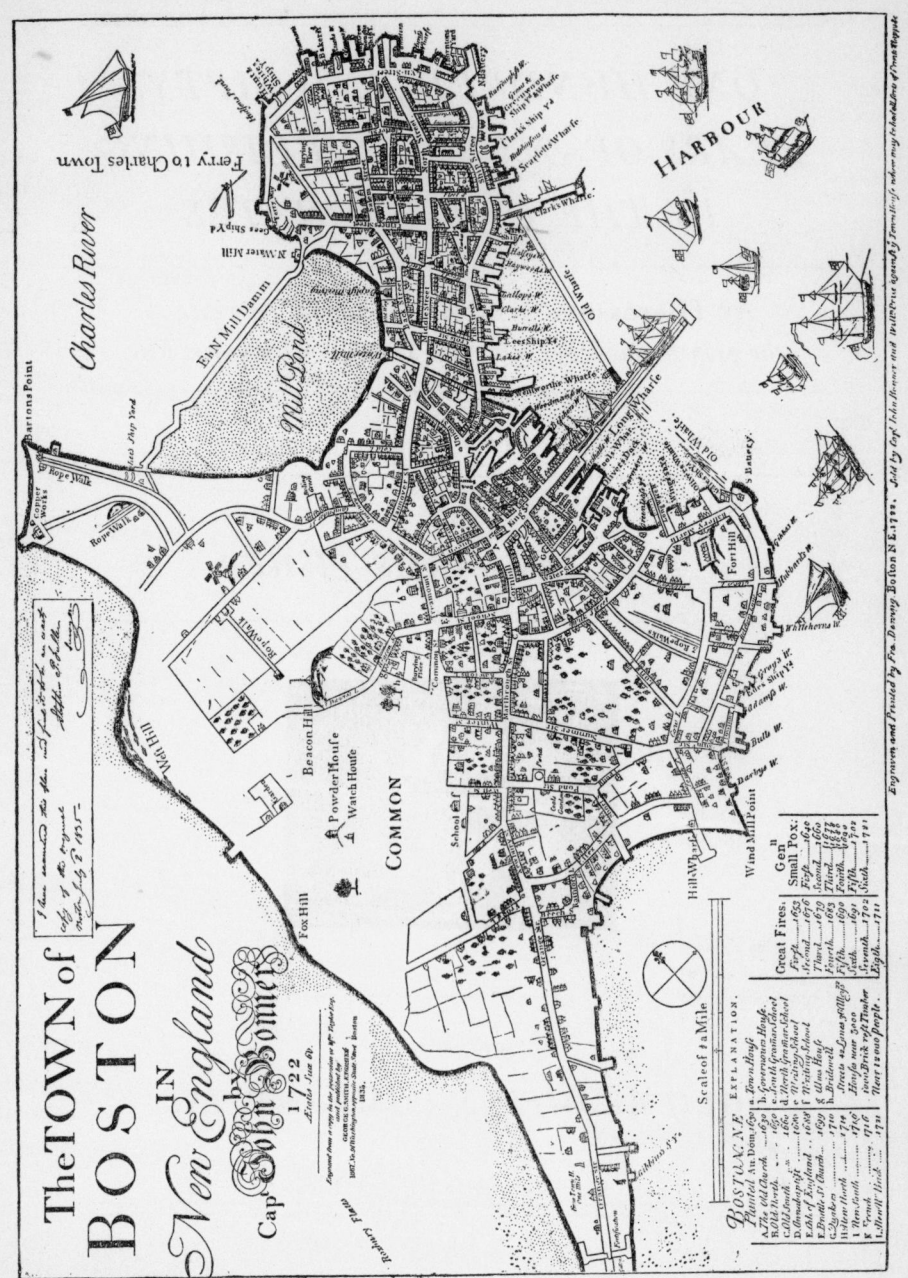

ONE HUNDRED AND FIFTY YEARS OF MUSIC PUBLISHING IN THE UNITED STATES

An Historical Sketch *with special reference to the pioneer publisher*, Oliver Ditson Company, Inc.

1783-1933

BY

WILLIAM ARMS FISHER

BOSTON
OLIVER DITSON COMPANY, INC.
1933

Copyright, MCMXXXIII, *by Oliver Ditson Company, Inc.*

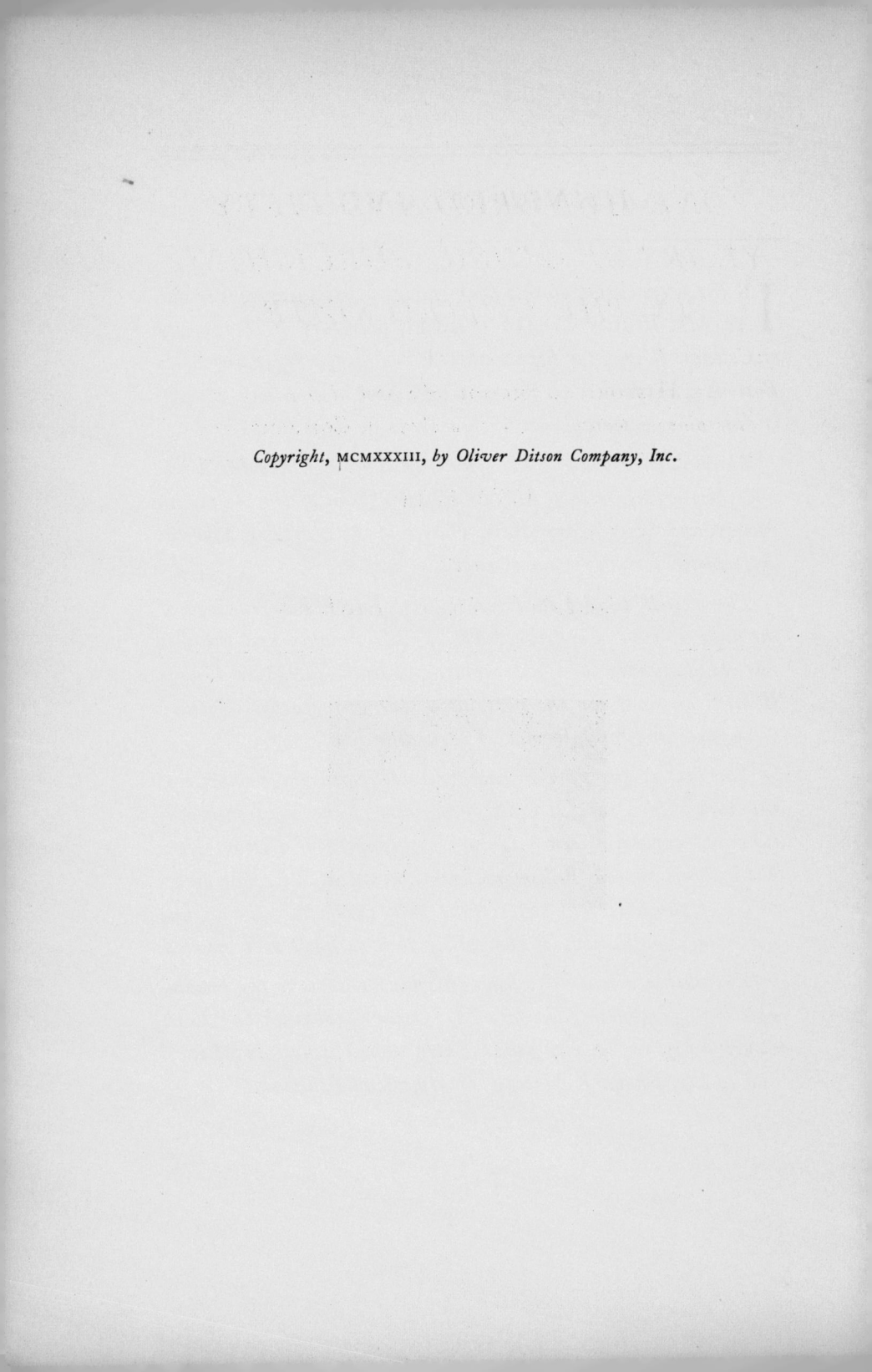

ACKNOWLEDGMENT

IN the preparation of this book special acknowledgment is due to Mr. Walter Kendall Watkins, Secretary of the Society of Colonial Wars, for his invaluable knowledge regarding early Boston. The chapter on "Some Early Book and Music-Shops" is due to his research.

Thanks are also due to Mr. Julius H. Tuttle of the Massachusetts Historical Society, Mr. Charles F. Read of the Bostonian Society, and Miss Mary Alden Thayer of the Harvard Musical Association for courtesies extended.

The author is also indebted to Mr. Joseph M. Jennings of the Old Corner Bookstore, Mr. J. M. Priaulx and the late Mr. H. J. Haney for illustrations, and to the late Mrs. George Whitefield Stone for the portrait of her grandfather, Gottlieb Graupner, and for information regarding him.

The text of the book is based directly upon the research of the author in a careful study of the files of the eighteenth century and early nineteenth century newspapers of Boston, New York, Philadelphia, Baltimore, and Charleston, S. C. The directories of the first four cities have been carefully collated, and surviving publications of the earlier periods have been studied.

The author also acknowledges his indebtedness to the invaluable bibliographies of the late Mr. Oscar G. Sonneck on "Early Concert-Life in America" and "Early Secular American Music," and to Mr. Frank J. Metcalf's "American Psalmody."

W. A. F.

CONTENTS

	Page
Acknowledgment	vii
List of Illustrations	xi
List of Music reproduced	xii
List of Portraits	xii
Boston Common, a prefatory note	xiii
Seventeenth Century, The	1
Eighteenth Century, The	6
First Music-shops and Publishers, The	23
Philadelphia Publishers	23
Baltimore Publishers	27
New York Publishers	28
Early Boston Book and Music-shops	32
Nineteenth Century, The (Boston)	45
Seventy Years More (Ditson)	71
Nineteenth Century and After, The	86
Philadelphia Publishers	86
Baltimore Publishers	93
New York Publishers	95
Boston Publishers	114
Cincinnati Publishers	128
Chicago Publishers	132
Conclusion	134
Index	137

LIST OF ILLUSTRATIONS

Buildings, Views, and Maps

	Page
Beacon Hill and Boston Common in 1838	54
Bonner's Map of Boston in 1722	Frontispiece
Boston from Pemberton Hill in 1816	41
Boston Common and Vicinity in 1722, from Bonner's Map	83
Boston Common in 1804, from the painting by Dobbins	xiii
Boston Common and State House about 1820	45
Boston Common and State House in 1830, from the water-color by George Harvey	44
Boston Common and Public Gardens about 1850, bird's-eye view	63
Common Street (Tremont Street) in 1798, Robertson's view of	135
Concert Hall, Hanover Street, Boston	17
Ditson Buildings, various	56, 72, 73, 77, 78, 84, 85
Great Organ in Music Hall, Boston	67
Holden's Organ	15
House in which Jenny Lind was married	66
King's Chapel, Boston, about 1865	48
Old Corner Bookstore, Boston, about 1837	53
Providence and Worcester railroads, Intersection of	54
State House, old, Boston, in 1791	22
State House and State Street in 1801	32
Tremont Street, Boston, March, 1918	82
Washington Street, Boston, West side in 1845	54, 55

Music

	Page
Adams and Liberty, from *Boston Musical Miscellany*, 1815	38
Cambridge Short Tune, from *Bay Psalm Book*, 14th edition, 1709	3
Hollis Street, from Billings' *New England Psalm Singer*, 1770	13
Medfield Tune, from *New England Psalm Singer*, 1770	13
Windsor Tune, from *Bay Psalm Book*, 9th edition, 1698	3
Windsor Tune, from *Bay Psalm Book*, 14th edition, 1709	3
Windsor Tune, from Walter's *Grounds and Rules of Musick*, 1721	7
York Tune, from *Bay Psalm Book*, 9th edition, 1698	3
York Tune, from Walter's *Grounds and Rules of Musick*, 1721	7

Portraits

	Page		Page
Buck, Dudley	70	Higginson, Henry Lee	64
Carreño, Teresa	67	Lang, B. J.	68
Church, John	71	Lind, Jenny	66
Ditson, Charles Healy	79	Paine, John K.	70
Ditson, Oliver	76	Presser, Theodore	90
Dwight, John S.	65	Rudersdorff, Hermine	69
Eichberg, Julius	68	Schirmer, Gustav	103
Fischer, Carl	106	Schirmer, Gustave, Jr.	122
Graupner, Gottlieb	45	Schmidt, Arthur P.	119
Grisi, Giulia	66	Urso, Camilla	67
Haynes, John C.	77	Wood, B. F.	125
Healy, P. J.	71	Zerrahn, Carl	64

BOSTON COMMON

A PREFATORY NOTE

THE buildings that face Boston Common look out upon open acres set in the very heart of a city that has grown great about them.

On or near the Common much of interest in American history has occurred, great men have walked there and near its borders great deeds have been done.

Near the southeast corner of the Common begins the Long Path that leads to Joy Street, made unforgettable through the charm of the *Autocrat of the Breakfast Table;* and, when Holmes was a youth of fifteen, General Lafayette was escorted with pomp along Tremont

Street, a throng of school children on the Common welcoming the hero by singing *The Marseillaise,* one of the young singers being Wendell Phillips. Now the broad walk along the Tremont Street side of the Common is known as Lafayette Mall.

It may have been nine years earlier that young Emerson is remembered to have driven the family cow down Beacon Street along the Common to an adjoining pasture, for it was not until 1833 that cows were excluded on complaint of the ladies. The boys always have used and still claim part of the Common as a playground, and Oliver Ditson, whose father's home still stands on Beacon Hill, played there, too, a hundred years ago.

On the knoll where the tall Soldiers' Monument stands, British artillery was stationed during the siege of Boston and, in the years preceding, British troops delighted in shocking religious Bostonians by racing horses on the Common on Sunday or causing their bands to play *Yankee Doodle* outside church doors.

The waters of the Back Bay once lapped the Common's marshy edge, and near the corner of Beacon and Charles Streets, where Blaxton had his wharf, the British troops, on the night of April 18, 1775, took their boats on the eve of the battle of Lexington, and with muffled oars rowed to the Cambridge shore; and in the little triangular burying ground, near the corner of Tremont and Boylston Streets, are graves of British soldiers killed at Bunker Hill. Somewhere in the same enclosure is the unmarked grave of the patriot composer, William Billings.

Across the Charles River, when the provincial troops were quartered in the churches and college buildings of Cambridge, they took down the leaden window-weights and organ pipes of Christ Church to mould them into bullets used at Bunker Hill; and near this same church, on July 3, General Washington took command of the levies assembled there preparatory to the siege of Boston.

Directly across the Common, near the corner of Beacon and Spruce Streets, long ago stood the hut and orchard of the Hermit of Shawmut, the Rev. William Blaxton, the first inhabitant, and it was from him that the Town of Boston, in 1634, bought for £30 all his rights in the peninsula, reserving forty-four acres as Commons for the freemen of the town for a "trayning field" and for "the feeding of cattell."

In its vicinity were issued the first book printed in America, the first treatise on singing, the first printed music, the first music instruction book, and the first book wholly of American composition.

Not far from it the first singing school was held, the first organ erected, the first spinet built, the first public concert advertised, the pioneer orchestra organized, the first complete performance of an oratorio given, and at the northeastern corner of the Common, in Park Street Church, *My Country, 'tis of thee* was for the first time sung.

As inheritors of so significant a past, it is only right to acknowledge this debt on the one hundred and fiftieth anniversary of the founding of Boston's oldest music-publishing house, the oldest in the United States. As the text will show, this historic house is also linked directly to the beginnings of music-publishing in Philadelphia, Baltimore, New York, Chicago, and Cincinnati. This sketch has therefore been broadened to include the chief publishers in the country, and to link the forgotten names of those who in the past struggled, lost or won, to the men who are carrying on in the living present.

Wm Arms Fisher

Boston, February 22, 1933.*

---

*Fifteen years ago to a day the author completed the manuscript of his *Notes on Music in Old Boston*, published in 1918. The new book is a revision and extension of the earlier work, broadening its scope and excluding many pages no longer relevant.

THE SEVENTEENTH CENTURY

Between the pioneer settlements at Jamestown in 1607, Plymouth in 1620, and Boston in 1630, and the establishing of music-publishing as a definite business, more than one hundred and fifty years elapsed. If the rough company of men that settled Jamestown and well-nigh perished in the attempt brought any music with them, it must have been only the memory of a few English folksongs, a sea-song or two, and possibly the tunes of a few hymns.

The Mayflower Pilgrims of 1620 brought to Plymouth their own psalter, translated for them by the scholarly Henry Ainsworth, and the forty-eight unharmonized tunes bound with it. This was first published in Amsterdam in 1612. Of other music brought to Plymouth Colony there is no record. The Ainsworth Psalter was used by the Pilgrims even after the Colony was merged with Massachusetts Bay in 1691.

When the small group of Hollanders that settled New Amsterdam began to hold the services of the Dutch Reformed Church in 1628, they sang the Psalms in unison from the diamond-shaped notes of the Dutch psalter, printed in Amsterdam; and in 1664 the Dutch Company sent out a schoolmaster and chorister to lead them.

The Puritan fleet of eleven ships that anchored in

Charlestown harbor in July, 1630, and under Governor Winthrop settled Boston-town, brought with them the psalter of Sternhold and Hopkins which dominated the English field for a century after its publication in 1562. As this first group of settlers included many clergymen and men of education and fortune, they doubtless brought with them a few copies of the new and important psalter of Thomas Ravenscroft, which had grown in favor since its issue in 1621. Its four-part harmonizations of the most used tunes became the musical authority of the period.

The stiff and ungainly diction of Sternhold and Hopkins' "authorized version" of the Psalms brought its own reaction, and the spirit of independence of the mother-country, that from the first was manifest, led the Puritan divines of Boston, Roxbury, and Dorchester to prepare a new metrical version of the Psalms. Known as *The Bay Pfalm Book*, and printed in Cambridge, Massachusetts, in 1640, it was, with the exception of an almanac, the first book printed in the American Colonies. It contained no music, however. The five or six tunes then in use, when noted at all, were written in the back of the psalm-books. Many congregations had but three or four tunes they could sing passably, for singing by rote was the custom, the Psalms being "lined out" by the deacon.

If, as has been stated, music was printed about 1690 to be appended to the psalm-books, no specimens have survived; and it was not until 1698, after an interval of fifty-eight years, that the ninth edition of *The Bay Pfalm Book*, printed in Boston, contained thirteen tunes in two-part harmony. This crudely-printed book, without bars except at the end of each line, is the oldest existing music of American imprint. The diamond-shaped notes were cut on wood, which will explain the crude appearance of the page reproduced below at the left. A page from the fourteenth edition, issued in 1709, is given at the right. The latter edition contains the melodies only of twelve tunes, and in still later editions music disappears.

The custom of reading each line of a Psalm before it was sung was instituted by the Reformers in England at a time when few in the congregations had books and few could read them. The practice of "lining out" was transplanted to Massachusetts Bay and must have been taken up at an early date, for books were scarce, the music was without any instrumental support, the few that could sing by note gradually died out, and the great majority sang by ear. It was only natural, therefore, that this crude and unmusical fashion should take root. The Psalms (there were then no hymns) were sung week after week in rotation without regard to their appropriateness to the sermon. The whole Psalm was sung through at one standing, a process that in the case of the longer Psalms took half an hour. In consequence, the few tunes used became well known and took on a certain sanctity and authority through long association. The introduction of new tunes was therefore strenuously opposed by the older people. Even the few tunes in use were sung differently and, there being no organs, they were often tortured beyond recognition by the addition of extemporized grace-notes in which no two singers agreed. These abuses lingered long in the eighteenth century, but they only duplicated current practices in the mother-country. As an evidence of progress it should be noted that Brattle Square Church on Dec. 20, 1699, "Voted unanimoufly that ye pfalms in our public Worfhip be fung without Reading line by line."

About the only evidence that merry-hearted singing and dancing were known in this early period is due to the fact that, as a seaport, Boston had many transient visitors, especially seamen, who indulged in such pleasure when ashore. Their conduct, made noisy no doubt by "much wafte of Wine and Beer," resulted, as early as 1646, in a law forbidding dancing in ordinaries and inns under penalty of five shillings for each offence.

In those days the very name "musician" was one of reproach but, stern as were the events and conditions of the period, surely some mother-hearts crooned lullabies as they rocked the cradle, or over their housework hummed in soft undertone some unforgotten folksong.

The Colonial literature of the last half of the seventeenth century, mostly an arid waste of forbidding theology, reflects the sombreness of the period. At the same time the growing material prosperity, coupled with echoes from the reaction against Puritanism the Restoration had brought in, the establishment of the Church of England in Boston, the presence of an aristocratic official British class, and other influences, had a mellowing effect and bigotry gradually weakened.

THE EIGHTEENTH CENTURY

In 1700 Boston had become a thrifty town of growing prosperity, with a population of perhaps 7,000. Two years before the first music of American imprint had appeared and with the advent of printed music the "new way" of singing by note came in.

The first book issued to meet this new want was entitled: "*A very plain and eafy Introduction to the Art of Singing Pfalm Tunes:* With the Cantus, or Trebles, of Twenty-eight Pfalm Tunes contrived in such a manner as that the Learner may attain the Skill of Singing them with the greateft eafe and Speed imaginable. By Rev. Mr. John Tufts. Price, *6d.* or *5s.* the doz."

This little book of a few pages, the first American book of sacred music published, was issued in Boston in 1714 or 1715, and was so successful, in spite of its substitution of letters for notes, as to reach its eleventh edition in 1744.

The innovation of note singing raised a great tempest among the older people, who regarded it as a plan to shut them out from one of the ordinances of worship. It was bitterly objected to as "Quakerifh and Popifh, and introductive of inftrumental mufick; the names given to the notes are blafphemous; it is a needlefs way fince their good Fathers are gone to heaven without it; its admirers are a company of young upftarts; they fpend too much time about learning, and tarry out a-nights diforderly," with many other equally strenuous and weighty reasons.

One of the valiant defenders of the "new way" was the Rev. Thomas Walter of Roxbury, who brought out in 1721, *The Grounds and Rules of Mufick explained, or an introduction to the art of finging by note.* This, the first practical American instruction book, and said to be the first music printed with bar-lines in America, was from the press of J. Franklin, at a time when his younger brother Benjamin, then a lad of fifteen, was learning the printer's trade as his apprentice.

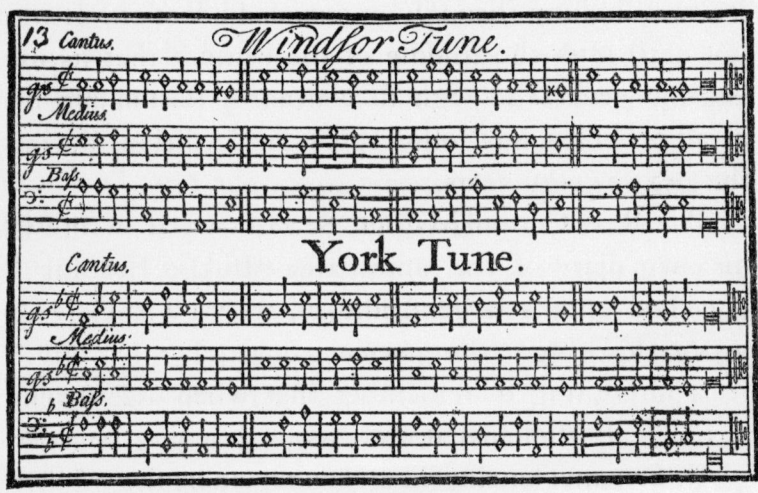

Page, reduced, from Walter's "Grounds and Rules of Musick"

The gradual victory of the advocates of the "new way" led to the establishment of singing schools, and as early as 1717 one is said to have existed in Boston. Judge Sewall records in his diary, under the date

[7]

March 16, 1721: "At night Dr. Mather preached in the School-House to the young Musicians, from Rev. 14.3. 'No man could learn that Song.'—House was full, and the Singing extraordinarily Excellent, such as has hardly been heard before in Boston. Sung four times out of Tate and Brady."

This is the earliest mention of the use of the "New Version," as Tate and Brady's metrical translation of the Psalms was called. First issued in London in 1696, its fluent and rhythmical paraphrase of the Psalms had greater appeal to the liberal minded than the more literal text of *The Bay Psalm Book*, to which the majority still clung through custom and affection. It was not until after the middle of the century that its use became general enough to warrant a Boston reprint in 1755. This was followed by rival editions during the next twenty years.

The Rev. Cotton Mather, Sewall's uncle, wrote in his own diary of the same date: "In the Evening I preached unto a large Auditory, where a Society of persons learning to Sing, began a quarterly solemnity." It is interesting to remember that when a few venturesome Bostonians, at the risk of learning ungodly songs, first met to sing in a class together, the mighty Handel, under the patronage of George the First, was dominating London's musical life, and the modest Bach was living the quiet life of *Kapellmeister* to an obscure German prince.

The music, or rather, the psalm singing (for there

was little else) was of course without the aid of instruments. When in 1713 Thomas Brattle, Esq., of Boston, willed the Brattle Square Church an organ, they declined it. He had provided, however, that in this event it was to be given to Queen's Chapel (known since the reign of Queen Anne as King's Chapel), but so great was the prejudice that the organ remained seven months in the porch of the church before it was unpacked. This instrument, set up in 1714, was the first pipe organ used in a church in New England, and it was bitterly denounced by Dr. Cotton Mather and other dignitaries of the day. In 1733 the second organ in New England was set up in Trinity Church, Newport. In 1790 the Brattle Square Church, having taken seventy-seven years to change its mind, ordered an organ built in London, but even then one of its leading members offered to reimburse the church for its outlay and to give a sum to the poor of Boston if they would allow him to have the unhallowed instrument thrown into the harbor. As late as 1814 there was no organ in Park Street Church, Boston, the singing being supported by a flute, bassoon and 'cello. Thomas Ryan of the Mendelssohn Quintette Club, who came to Boston in 1845, played the clarinet for two years in Father Streeter's Church in Hanover Street, the other instruments being a double-bass and ophicleide. There was then, he records, no organ in this and several other Boston churches.

    The earliest reference to the use of an organ in any church in the Colonies is to the organ in the gallery of Gloria Dei Church, the Swedish Lutheran Church, dedicated July 2, 1700, that still stands in Philadelphia. When the saintly Pietist, Justus Falckner, was ordained in this church on November 24, 1703, it is recorded that:

> "*The service was opened with a voluntary on the little organ in the gallery by Jonas, the organist, supplemented with instrumental music by the Mystics on the viol, hautboy, trombones, and kettle-drums.*"

This earlier record makes the Brattle organ of Boston the second to be used in church services in the Colonies. As to which of these organs crossed the Atlantic first there is at present no proof, although it is not improbable that the wealthy Mr. Brattle may have brought his organ from London on his return trip in October, 1689.

In 1727 music-loving William Burnet, Governor of New York, gave an organ to the Low Dutch Reformed Church of New York and appointed Hendrick M. Koek as organist. The fourth organ of record was that purchased in 1728 from Ludovic Sprögell, the mystic, for Christ Church, Philadelphia. The fifth organ, as far as known, was that in St. Philip's Church, Charleston, S. C. The church was built in 1723, but the records are silent as to when the organ was set up. We only know that John Salter was its organist as early as March, 1732. He may have filled this position earlier.

The sixth organ was that set up in Trinity Church,

Newport, R. I., in 1733, the gift of Bishop Berkeley, the philosopher. The records of old Petsworth Church in Gloucester County, Virginia, show that "great subcriptions" were made in 1735 for the purchase of an organ. If set up in this year the organ would rank seventh or eighth in order, for Trinity Church, Boston, in this same year had "A neat little organ, prettily embellished." The organ brought from Newport, R. I., and erected in Christ Church, Boston, in 1736, would be the ninth, while the organ built by Johann G. Klemm of Philadelphia in 1741 for Trinity Church, New York, would be the tenth Colonial organ of record. It should be remembered that, with one possible exception, these early organs were without pedals for, although invented in Germany in the early fifteenth century, pedals were not introduced in England until near the close of the eighteenth century.

In 1764 Josiah Flagg of Boston, published *A Collection of the beſt Pſalm Tunes, in two, three, and four-parts*, the largest collection up to this time printed in New England. This volume of about eighty small oblong pages is notable in that for the first time light music was intermingled with psalm-tunes, and because the music was engraved with skill by the noted silversmith, Paul Revere — and further, that it was printed on paper made in the Colonies, which fact Mr. Flagg hopes "will not diminiſh the value of the work in the eſtimation of any, but may in ſome degree recommend it, even to thoſe who have no peculiar reliſh for the muſic."

This Josiah Flagg was a man of energy and enthusiasm, and for some time the most important local musician. He gave concerts of quality, and as early as 1771 the name of Handel appears on his programs.

As some of the members of the Puritan congregation became more proficient in singing, they naturally drew together and later were assigned special seats. In this way choirs gradually came into existence before the sterner opposing faction realized the transition. Vocal collections increased in number and by the end of the eighteenth century nearly eighty had appeared in New England alone.

The first Philadelphia publication of historic importance was Rev. James Lyon's *Urania*, containing seventy wordless psalm-tunes, fourteen hymns, and twelve anthems, making it the largest collection of church music thus far published in the Colonies. The bulk of the music was taken from current English collections, but at least six of the tunes were by Lyon himself. It was issued to subscribers in 1761 or 1762.

As in the case of *Urania*, little of the music in the many collections issued at this time was original, although native composers began to appear. The first New Englander of note was the eccentric, one-eyed, snuff-taking tanner's apprentice, William Billings. He was born in Boston, October 7, 1746, four years after Handel produced *The Messiah* in Dublin, and ten years before Mozart saw the light in Salzburg. Billings' first book, *The New England Pfalm Singer*, appeared in the year of Beethoven's birth, 1770. Thus, one hundred and forty years after the founding of Boston, the first book of native music was issued, and with it the publishing of American composition may be said to begin. It contained one hundred and eight pages and presented one hundred and twenty tunes, and several anthems, as well as twenty-two pages of elementary instruction, and an essay on the nature and

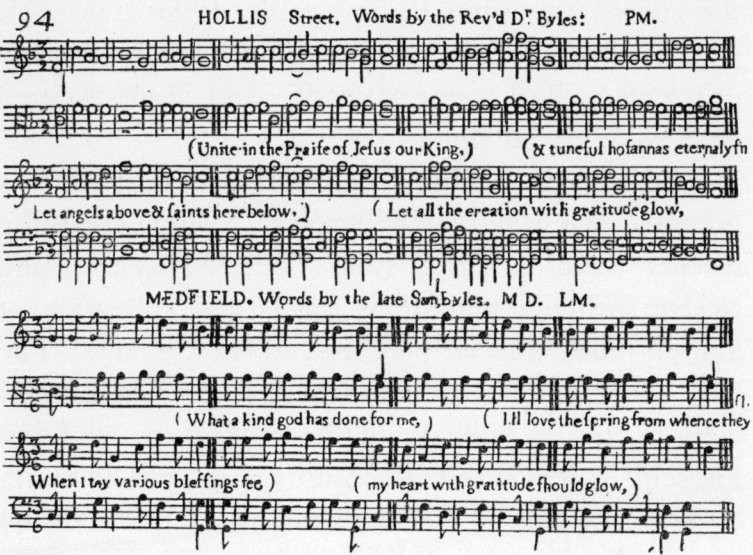

Page from Billings' "New England Psalm Singer"

properties of musical sound. In 1778 Billings published a revision and abridgment of his first book entitled *The Singing Mafter's Affistant*, which soon became known as "Billings Best." In his naïve preface to the new book, Billings characterizes his first book as "this infant production of my own Numb-Skull," and further on says,

[13]

"I have difcovered that many of the pieces in that Book were never worth my printing, or your infpection."

Billings' music with all its uncouthness was, in comparison with the prevailing style, melodic, cheerful and rhythmic. In 1779 he issued *Mufic in Miniature*, and two years later, *The Pfalm-Singer's Amufement*, which also became popular. His sixth and last book, *The Continental Harmony*, was published in 1794. He died in Boston, September 26, 1800. Billings is said to have been the first to introduce the violoncello in New England churches, as well as the first to use a pitch-pipe to "set the tune." The singing class of forty-eight residents of Stoughton, Massachusetts, he taught in 1774, was formally organized November 7, 1786, shortly after the Revolution, as the Stoughton Musical Society, and still exists.

The fuguing style of Billings' music and its crudities may now provoke a smile but, after a century and a half of the dull and monotonous drawling of a few threadbare psalm-tunes, the spirited style which Billings introduced must have delighted the young people of his day. He gave to local music a new meaning, a fresh impulse, a greater freedom.

Another notable figure in the musical life of this period was Oliver Holden, born in Shirley, Massachusetts, in 1765. He settled in Charlestown, Massachusetts, in 1788, as a carpenter and joiner, and then dropped his tools to become a music-teacher. He is remembered to this day by his stirring hymn tune,

Coronation, which appeared in *The American Harmony*, published by Holden, in 1792. He prospered, and his fine house in Pearl Street, Charlestown, where he wrote *Coronation*, is still standing. The little pipe organ he used is now in the custody of the Bostonian Society in the old State House. In 1797 Holden published *The Worcester Collection of Sacred Harmony*, which had a wide and long-continued influence. It was printed from movable types by Isaiah Thomas of Worcester, who advertised in the Boston *Independent Chronicle* of January 26, 1785, that he "has received from England a beautiful set of mufic types whereby he is enabled to print any kind of Church or other mufic in a neat and elegant manner, cheaper than heretofore done from copper and pewter plates. Specimens to be seen at Battelle's Bofton Book Store, State Street." (See p. 34.)

Holden's Organ and Portrait

In the latter half of the eighteenth century, because of the victory of choirs and singing schools over "the old way," books of music appeared in profusion. The secular spirit is most manifest in *The Columbian Song-*

ster and Free Mason's Pocket Companion, published by E. Larkin, No. 47 Cornhill, Boston, in 1798. "A collection of the neweſt and moſt celebrated Sentimental, Convivial, Humorous, Satirical, Paſtoral, Hunting, Sea and Maſonic ſongs, being the largeſt and beſt collection ever published in America." This collection, like many of its type, consisted of text only, the air to which each number fitted being named but not printed.

∴

While psalmody was predominant in the early musical life of Boston it must not be thought that music for recreation and entertainment had no place, for the first half of the eighteenth century brought to Boston men of rank in the British Navy and Army who were accustomed to the life of English and Continental society. Moreover, the various military expeditions to Canada against the French gave New England a taste of the roving life of the soldier and sailor. These conditions, together with increasing prosperity, naturally gave rise to a demand for public entertainment.

The first advertisement of a public concert in America, thus far discovered, appeared in the weekly *Boston News-Letter* of December 16-23, 1731: "There will be performed a *Concert of Muſic* on ſundry Inſtruments at Mr. Pelham's great Room, being the Houſe of the late Doctor Noyes near the Sun Tavern." The next concerts of record are those of November 23 and December 28, 1732, advertised in the *New England Weekly Journal* of November 13 and December 15, as "Conforts of Mufick performed on fundry inftruments at the Concert Room in Wing's Lane near the Town Dock." This was a room in the George Tavern on what is now Elm Street. The generosity of Peter Faneuil in giving the town Faneuil Hall, finished in 1742, furnished a room in 1744 for a vocal and instrumental concert. Ten years later, Gilbert Deblois, organist of King's Chapel, and his brother built a brick building on the east corner of Hanover and Court Streets. Their shop, the sign of the *Crown and Comb*, was on the ground floor. Above was a hall fitted in a handsome manner for concerts. This was known as "Concert Hall" and for nearly a century was the resort of Bostonians on pleasure bent. It was torn down in 1869 when Hanover Street was widened. The *Bofton Chronicle*, in November, 1768, advertises concerts at the "Mufic-Hall in Brattle Street, oppofite Dr. Cooper's Meeting-Houfe."

Concert Hall

Concerts at this period were advertised to begin at six o'clock, and the tickets were usually half a dollar or "two shillings — lawful money." At a concert of sacred music performed at the Stone Chapel (King's Chapel), December 11, 1789, under the direction of Mr. William Selby, the chapel's organist, the choruses were by "The Independent Musical Society, the instrumental parts by a Society of Gentlemen, with the band of His Most Christian Majesty's Fleet." This William Selby, harpsichordist, organist, composer, music-teacher, active concert-manager, and during the stringency of the Revolution a grocer, was one of the chief figures in Boston's musical life between 1772 and his death in December, 1798.

Most of the early concerts seem to have been for the benefit of the poor of the town and were given by permission of the Selectmen. The name of Handel began to appear in 1770, and occurs not infrequently as the "late celebrated Mr. Handel." The French Revolution drove a number of musicians to the Colonies, and after 1793 programs in Boston and elsewhere were in consequence lighter in character.

Concert-giving in the pre-Revolution period consisted either of the sporadic efforts of more or less itinerant musicians to gain sustenance and public attention, or the attempts of music-lovers among the well-to-do to maintain strictly private concerts, usually concluded with a ball. Concerts, therefore, were then primarily social functions. The year 1783, when the treaty of Paris was signed, marked the resumption of normal activity in all lines, with an increase in concert-giving and an improvement in their quality.

As already noted, the first concert of record in the Colonies was that advertised in the *Boston News-Letter* of December 16-23, 1731, "to be held at Mr. Pelham's great Room." New York's first advertised concert was the *Consort of Musick, Vocal and Instrumental, for the Benefit of Mr. Pachelbel,* to be given on January 21, 1736. In Philadelphia, because of social conditions and religious prejudice, its public concerts prior to the Revolution were few in number. The first advertised concert was that of January 25, 1757—*A Concert of Music, under the direction of Mr. John Palma.* In Baltimore, concert-life did not begin until after the Revolution, when William Brown, the flutist, gave *A Concert of Instrumental Music* on January 30, 1784. Pleasure-loving Charleston, S. C., had an independent musical life of considerable importance. Its fashionable St. Coecilia Society was the nucleus of much musical activity, and the love of the theatre was less restricted by prejudice than in the towns of the North. Its first public concert of record was that given in mid-April, 1732, *A Consort of Musick at the Council Chamber, for the benefit of Mr. Salter.*

Although music in the churches had advanced greatly during the century, a sidelight is thrown upon it by a writer in the *American Apollo* of April 20, 1792. In "Lines written, rather out of temper, on a Pannel in one of the Pews of S—m Church," he says:

"*Could poor King David but for once
To S—m Church repair,*

*And hear his Pſalms thus warbled out,
Good Lord, how he would ſwear!"*

The dawn of a polite interest in music as a social accomplishment is indicated by the first advertisements of the teaching of music. These appeared in the newspapers of Boston in 1712, Philadelphia in 1730, Charles-town, S. C. in 1733, and in New York in 1745. In this early period, musicians were regarded more or less as vagabonds, and had little opportunity beyond playing the fiddle for dancing, and teaching the flute to a few gentlemen amateurs, or the spinet to young ladies in aristocratic families. After the Revolution music-teachers gradually increased in number and favor and instrumental music began to find a place in the home. A French visitor, Brissot de Warville, writing in 1788 regarding Bostonians, says: "Music, which their teachers formerly proscribed as a diabolical art, begins to make part of their education. In some houses you hear the forte-piano. This art, it is true, is still in its infancy."

The first publication of a separate song in the Colonies was advertised, as here given, in the *Boston Chronicle* of August 29, 1768, and in other papers:

It is to be regretted that no copy of this

The NEW and FAVOURITE
LIBERTY SONG,
In FREEDOM we're Born, &c.
Neatly engraved on COPPER-PLATE, the ſize of half a ſheet of Paper,
Set to MUSIC for the VOICE,
And to which is alſo added,
A SET of NOTES adapted to the
GERMAN FLUTE and VIOLIN,
Is juſt publiſhed and to be SOLD at the
LONDON Book-ſtore, King-ſtreet, Boſton,
Price SIXPENCE Lawful ſingle, and
FOURSHILLINGS Lawful, the dozen.

[20]

initial "Song for American Freedom" has yet come to light, for it was not only the first patriotic song published, but the first separately printed piece of sheet music issued. The text was written in the troubled year of 1768, by John Dickinson, the Philadelphia patriot known as "the penman of the Revolution." Set to the music of the familiar song, *Hearts of Oak*, written in 1759 by the English composer, William Boyce, it was sung throughout the Colonies, for the words were widely printed, north and south.

The publication of secular music prior to the Revolution was very slight; the years of war put a stop to even this, and the period of readjustment and struggle for National Government that followed was equally unfavorable. The opening of the first Congress in 1789 marked the turning point, the old order faded out and in this very year secular music-publishing took a start in Boston and Philadelphia, while New York became active in 1793.

Much of the secular music issued was patriotic, or echoed passing events, the bulk of it being altogether ephemeral. Naturally much English music was reprinted, chiefly the songs of Hook, Dibdin, Shield, and Storace. Reprints of the music of Haydn, Gluck, Pleyel, Mozart, and Handel were few in number although their names appear with increasing frequency on concert programs.

While Boston was behind Philadelphia and New York in the publication of secular music, in the output of sacred music it greatly exceeded the rest of the country, while the neighboring towns of Dedham, Newburyport, Salem, Northampton, and Worcester added their quota.

It was not until the close of the century that music-shops, under the name of "magazines" or "emporiums," began to appear, but the constant removals of these early music and book-shops and the frequency with which they changed hands suggest a somewhat precarious existence for the pioneers.

THE FIRST MUSIC-SHOPS AND PUBLISHERS

PRIOR to the Revolution such music as was sold was to be had of book-shops and stationers, while the publishing of music was the private affair of the composer usually backed by subscriptions. Psalm-books and church music were distributed by the printers of the books, but the cost of publication was borne by the composers or compilers. In other words, before 1786 there were, with a single exception, no music-shops nor any music-publishers as such. This single exception was in Philadelphia.

PHILADELPHIA PUBLISHERS

From 1750 the musical life of this city advanced rapidly and as in 1760 and even in 1800 it was the largest city in the country, as well as its political center, it is only natural that the first music-shop of record in the country should be opened there. This was opened late in 1759 by Michael Hillegas, at his house in Second Street, where he kept quite an extensive assortment of instruments, music, and music-paper. His stock of music as advertised in the *Pennsylvania Gazette* of January 5, 1764 is remarkable, but there is no record of his publishing any music. This shop was not long continued after 1765, for Hillegas was a man of affairs and became so important as to hold office as the first Treasurer of the United States.

The first publishing of music in Philadelphia at the composer's risk and expense was by Thomas Dobson, who, from 1791 until 1798 or 1799, was a printer and book-seller at 41 North Second Street. In August, 1787, he printed for the arranger and compiler, Alexander Reinagle, a *Select Collection of the most favorite Scot's tunes* with variations for the pianoforte or harpsichord. In 1789 Dobson printed another book for him — a *Collection of Favorite Songs*. Reinagle's abilities as pianist, composer, and theatrical manager made him prominent in the musical life of Philadelphia for more than a decade from 1786.

It was Dobson who also printed what, so far as known, was the first publication of secular music by an American-born composer, the book of *Seven songs for the Harpsichord or forte piano* by Francis Hopkinson, jurist, poet, painter, musician, and man of affairs, whose claim to be the first native American composer seems now well established. This oblong, quarto book of eleven engraved music-pages, containing *eight* songs, was advertised in the *Federal Gazette* of November 29, 1788, as "This day published and to be sold by Thomas Dobson, at the Stone House in Second Street, between Chestnut and Market Streets."

Dobson, however, was a stationer and book-printer, and the first Philadelphia publisher of music only was the firm of Moller & Capron, who had a music and piano store combined with a music-school at 163 North Third Street, and in the *Federal Gazette* of March, 1793, advertised for subscribers to a series of monthly numbers, of six pages each, to contain all "the newest vocal and instrumental music." At least three such numbers were issued. John C. Moller, a German organist, pianist, and composer, appeared in New York concerts in 1790 as a harpsichordist, and came to Philadelphia the same year; while Henry Capron was a French 'cellist and composer of prominence who first appears in Philadelphia's concert life in 1785. The firm, however, was short-lived and the credit of establishing music-publishing in Philadelphia must be given to Benjamin Carr, the English singer, pianist, organist, conductor, and composer, a well-schooled, all-round musician of fine breeding, and a pupil of Dr. Samuel Arnold, who, from his arrival in Philadelphia in 1793, at the age of twenty-four, to his death on May 24, 1831, was a vigorous force in the musical life of the city.

Under the name of B. Carr & Co., he opened a "Musical Repository," "for the sale of music and musical instruments of all kinds," in July, 1793, at 136 High Street, removing in November of the same year to 122 Market Street, where, after the autumn of 1794, Carr carried on the business alone. Apparently the business ceased about 1800, though for a time thereafter he had as partner the Scotch 'cellist, J. G. Schetky, under the firm name Carr & Schetky. Besides original songs by Carr and Raynor Taylor of Philadelphia, songs by

Dibdin, Hook, Shield, Storace, Dr. Arnold, and Dr. Jackson were reprinted, together with pieces for the pianoforte and "Elegant extracts" for the flute or violin. In April, 1798, Carr issued the original edition of *Hail! Columbia;* and in 1799 he advertises the publication of Haydn's *Canzonets*, the first American edition, and a song by Mozart, whose name was then little known.

John Aitken, the music-engraver, had for a while a music-store on South Third Street, and published some music. In 1793 George E. Blake came over from England, taught the flute and clarinet, and later published music. Another musician who tried his hand at publishing was Robert Shaw, a ballad-singer, oboist, bassoonist, and composer, who kept a music-shop in 1794 as Shaw & Co., and with various changes and removals continued until 1803.

In November, 1794, George Willig opened his "Musical magazine" "at 163 North Third Street, in the house formerly occupied by Mr. Moller." In March, 1795, we find him at 165 Market Street, and though publishing songs then in vogue he seems to have given more attention than his rivals to instrumental music. Willig outlasted his early contemporaries and continued selling and publishing music in Philadelphia until his business was absorbed by Lee & Walker in 1856. This large concern was active until 1875, when their catalog and stock were purchased by Oliver Ditson & Co. of Boston, thus linking the Ditson house to the beginnings of music-publishing in Philadelphia.

BALTIMORE PUBLISHERS

The wave that initiated music-publishing as a separate business in this country reached the centers of population almost simultaneously. In the closing decade of the eighteenth century Baltimore grew rapidly, for its population increased from 13,500 in 1790 to 26,500 in 1800.

While credit has just been given to Benjamin Carr as a pioneer publisher in Philadelphia, similar credit must be given to Joseph Carr, his father, who had been a music-publisher at Middle Row, Holborn, in London, for initiating music-publishing in Baltimore but a year later. He opened his Musical Repository on Market Street, near Gay Street, in 1794, and the *Maryland Journal* of August 6, 1794, advertises "J. Carr, Music Importer, lately from London, Respectfully informs the public that he has opened a Store entirely in the Musical line, and has for SALE, Finger and barrel organs, double and single key'd harpsichords; piano fortes and common guitars." He started out bravely as a dealer in music and musical instruments, but in 1795 he also advertises blankets, looking-glasses, and black beaver hats. From 1795 J. Carr's address was No. 6 Gay Street. The Directory of 1807 locates him at 48 Baltimore Street. His two most notable publications, from an historic point of view, were Francis Hopkinson's *Ode from Ossian's Poems*, and the first edition of *The Star-Spangled Banner* "(adpd. and arrd. by T.C.)", in other words, adapted and arranged by

[27]

Thomas Carr, his son. This son was a well-trained musician, and from 1798 to 1811 the organist of Christ Church. As the pioneer publishing-house of Carr carried on, through its successors, into the middle of the nineteenth century, its story is continued in a later chapter.

NEW YORK PUBLISHERS

At the beginning of the last decade of the eighteenth century the proud city at the mouth of the Hudson had, according to the first census (1790), a population of 33,131, while Philadelphia listed 42,444, but by 1810 New York had taken the lead it has since maintained. Which of these two cities can claim priority in establishing a regular publisher of music is somewhat in doubt.

In May, 1786, John Jacob Astor opened a stock of "Musical instruments, music-books, and papers, and every other article in the musical line." This venture was but temporary, a mere interlude before Mr. Astor went into the fur business upon which his fortune was founded.

As early as January, 1787, George Gilfert (Gifford, Giffert), the violin player, kept a Musical Magazine, in other words a music-shop. He was also organist of the New Dutch Church, kept a tavern, and then a boarding-house. In January, 1795, he began to publish music, the firm continuing until 1814.

In January, 1790, P. A. von Hagen, who a few

years later became Boston's first publisher of secular music, advertised instruments and music for sale at his lodgings.

Early in 1793 young Benjamin Carr, singer, organist, and composer, and son of the London music-publisher, Joseph Carr, arrived in New York. He seems to have opened a music-shop almost immediately, for in April he advertised *Freedom Triumphant*, a new song, just published by B. Carr, No. 131 William Street. In July he moved to Philadelphia where, as already stated, he opened a Musical Repository. For awhile he maintained both shops, but in 1797 he sold his New York branch to James Hewitt and confined his activities to the Quaker city, where he played an important part in its musical life.

In July, 1793, James Harrison opened a music-store at No. 38 Maiden Lane, in August he announced the issue of two songs, and in December the opening of a "Musical Circulating Library," the first of its kind, so far as known.

In 1792 James Hewitt, the English composer, conductor, and violinist arrived from London in company with Gehot, Bergman, Young, and Phillips as "Professors of music from the Opera house, Hanover Square, and Professional Concerts under the direction of Haydn, Pleyel, etc., London." In 1794 he began to publish music, although it was not until four years later that he was fully established as a publisher at 131 William Street. In 1797 he took over the New York store of Benjamin Carr. He was still in business in 1811 at 59 Maiden Lane, but the directories of 1818 and 1819 list him only as "Musician." A few years later he went to Boston with his son James L. Hewitt and died there in 1827.

Another pioneer publisher was John Paff who had a music-store at 112 Broadway in 1798, and as John & M. Paff, and later (1811) without this relative, continued until 1817.

But little of the published eighteenth century music has survived. Some of it is doubtless still hidden in dusty attics and old trunks, but most of it went long ago to the junk-man or the dust-heap. These pioneer publishers naturally issued the music then in demand, the bulk of it English songs, many of them taken from the London Ballad-Operas of Arne, Arnold, Attwood, Dibdin, Hook, Kelly, Linley, Reeve, Shield, Storace, and others. These operettas and pasticcios were well performed in the chief cities by the itinerant Old American Company and its successors and rivals in the days when nearly every actor and actress was a singer and every singer an actor. These well-routined groups were mostly from London and included such stars as Mrs. Pownall, not only a great actress but a singer of genuine artistry; the versatile and popular John Hodgkinson; his skilled wife Arabella Brett; the accomplished Miss Broadhurst; the famous Mrs. Oldmixon; the beautiful Maria Storer; the sterling character-actor Thomas Wignell, and others.

An idea of the character and volume of the secular music published in the eighteenth century may be gained from an analysis of the late Oscar Sonneck's valuable monograph, *Early Secular American Music.*

Basing his study on a careful examination of the files of available eighteenth century American newspapers and magazines, surviving music and books to be found in our chief libraries, and the few bibliographical works covering the period, Mr. Sonneck printed a list of titles not only of secular music advertised as published or announced for publication, but the titles of works performed prior to January 1, 1800, whether known to be published in this country or not.

By confining the items to music and books known to have been published, the following figures summarize the issue of secular music in the eighteenth century in Boston, New York, Philadelphia, Baltimore, and Charleston:

a. Books and Collections of Music (secular only)	46
*b. Published in the few magazines of the period	68
c. Separate publications of sheet music	329
Total	443

Of these 443 titles but three were published prior to 1780, and the bulk of the items were issued in the closing seven years of the century.

**Massachusetts Magazine* and *Boston Magazine*, the *New York Magazine*, and the *Musical Asylum* of Philadelphia.

EARLY BOSTON BOOK AND MUSIC-SHOPS

In the early days there was neither the population nor the publication to sustain music-shops. Books of psalmody and the few instruction books were as a rule issued to subscribers and distributed by the author or compiler himself, by his printer, or through book-sellers. The latter were the chief purveyors of music and music-books and continued to be so until the close of the eighteenth century. In fact, this combination of book-selling and music-selling carried well over into the first third of the nineteenth century, when it was fre-

State Street in 1801

quently mixed with the sale of umbrellas and parasols, together with even more mundane articles.

The sale of music was not even confined to bookstores, for the *Boston Gazette* of January 12, 1767, advertises that "*Tanfur's Royal Melody Compleat*, the laſt and beſt Edition, may be had at John Perkins's Shop in Union Street. N. B. At the ſame Place may be had a large aſſortment of Paper Hangings for Rooms."

A prominent mid-century book-shop was the *London Book-Store*, located on the north side of King Street (now State Street), across from the old State House. In 1762 it was kept by James Rivington, afterwards a New York publisher, and then by Rivington and Miller. In 1765 it was kept by John Mein, who had been a book-seller in Edinburgh. His circulating library consisted of above 1200 volumes "in most branches of polite literature, arts and sciences." The character of his music stock is shown by the advertisement (part of a full column ad.) reproduced from the *Boston Gazette* of July 17, 1766.

In 1769 Mein was mobbed for his utterances in favor of the British Government in

April Magazines,
1s lawful each, juſt arrived in the LYDIA, Captain SLOT, to be had of

John Mein,
At the London Book Store, King-ſtreet, Boſton;

Williams's Univerſal Pſalmodiſt, *a new* Edition carefully correcled and improved, with an Addition of near 40 new Tunes and Anthems that have met with univerſal Approbation among the muſical Societies.
Knapps new Set of Pſalms and Anthems, *with a Paſtoral Hymn by the famous Mr. Addiſon*
Arnold's Complete Pſalmodiſt, or Pſalm ſinger's Companion.
—— Church Muſic reformed
—— Leiceſterſhire Harmony
Green's Body of Pſalmody

his paper the *Boston Chronicle*, and his failure two years later gave young Henry Knox his opportunity, for he opened a new *London Book-Store* on Cornhill (Washington Street), where the office of the *Boston Globe* now stands. Knox was popular, and his shop became a great resort for British officers and Tory ladies. When the loyal Knox left town at the outbreak of the Revolution in April, 1775, to attain renown as a General and later as Secretary of War, his store was robbed, pillaged of its stock by the Royalists and his business as a bookseller ended.

During the war, business was dislocated, foreign importation of books and music was suspended and bookselling was reduced to the small output of a few printers of American books.

After the war, in 1783, Colonel Ebenezer Battelle, a native of Dedham, opened at No. 8 State Street (no longer King Street) the *Boston Book-Store*. His music stock is indicated in the advertisement reproduced here from the *Massachusetts Centinel* of November 6, 1784.

> MUSICK.
> Lately received, and SOLD at
> E. BATTELLE's Book-Store,
> STATE-STREET,
> A VALUABLE Collection of MUSICK BOOKS, consisting of Airs, Songs, Country-Dances, Minuets and Marches. —Symphonies, Quartellos, Concertos, Sonatas, Divertimentos, Duettos, Solos, Trios, Oratorios, &c. for the Organ, Harpsichord, Clarinett, French-Horn, Hautboy, Flute, Violin, Violincello, Harp, Piano-Forte, Voice, &c.
> PSALMODY.
> Massachusetts Harmony.
> Law's elect Harmony.
> ———'s Collection of Hymns,
> ———'s Rules of Psalmody with Tunes and Chaunts annexed.
> ———'s Select tunes.
> N. B. Books and Stationary as usual.

Colonel Battelle was a graduate of Harvard, served during the Revolution in the Massachusetts Militia, was made Captain in 1778, Major in 1780 and Colonel of the Boston Regiment in 1784. His military proclivities interfered with his book business, which did not prove profitable, especially under the depreciation of Continental currency, for $4,000 in bills of credit were worth but $100 in silver. On February 1, 1785, Battelle moved to 10 Marlboro Street, but sold out his music and circulating library at 8 State Street to Benjamin Guild. In 1788, as a pioneer member of the Ohio Company, he settled at Marietta, and died in Newport, Ohio, in 1815.

In the *Independent Chronicle* of December 1, 1785, Guild advertises his latest importations.

The following year Guild moved his bookstore to 59 Cornhill, "First door South of the Old-Brick Meeting-House," according to his advertisements in October, 1786.

After Guild's death, in 1792, his administrator, William Pinson Blake, continued the business at 59 Cornhill, being succeeded in 1796 by William Pelham, at the same location where

Imported, in the last vessel from London, AND NOW SELLING, by
Benjamin Guild,
At the BOSTON BOOK-STORE,
No. 8, STATE-STREET,

GUTHRIE'S
Geographical Grammar, published last May, with large additions and improvements,
Elegant Extracts, new edition,
Buchan's Family Physician, new edition,
Pulpit and family folio Bibles, with notes and cuts,
Peregrine Pickle,
Tristram Shandy,
Sentimental Journey;
Tom Jones,
Gill Blas,
Churchill's Poems,
Goldsmith's Essays,
Swift's Polite Conversation,
Thomson's Seasons,
Gay's Fables,
Hudibras,
Shenstone's Poetical Works
Moore's Fables,
Roderick Random,
Joseph Andrews,
Paradise Lost.

Also, may be had, (besides a general assortment of books)
The Massachusetts Register; Thomas's, Bickerstaff's, George's, Low's and Weatherwise's Almanacks, for 1786; a large and elegant assortment of Account and other Blank-Books; Alphabets; Visiting Cards; Ink and Ink-Powder; Ink-Stands; Pencils; counting-house and other Penknives; Slates; cases of Surveying Instruments; ivory Folders; Spy-Glasses; Money-Scales; pocket-Books, Maps, Charts; and a great variety of other articles.

☞ A few patent LAMPS.

his relative, William Price, previously lived and had a book-store.

William Pelham, born in Williamsburg, Virginia, in 1759, was a grandson of the Peter Pelham who married Mary Copley, mother of the painter, John Singleton Copley. The building at 59 Cornhill (now 219 Washington Street), the original site of Thompson's Spa of today, had been purchased in 1736 by William Price, who published in 1743 his *View of Boston*. Price also dealt in music, for in 1769 he advertises on his map of Boston, "Flutes, Hautboys & Violins, Strings, Muſical Books, Songs, &c."

With the exception of the *Liberty Song*, issued in September, 1768, by the London Book Store (see p. 20), none of the Boston shops thus far mentioned published music. Although the Puritan town greatly exceeded all other sections in the issue of psalmody, it lagged behind both Philadelphia and New York in the issue of secular music and in establishing a regular music-publisher.

Boston's first established music-publisher was the organist, pianist, violinist, composer, and conductor, Peter Albrecht von Hagen, of Rotterdam and London. He came to Charleston, S. C., in 1774, but the outbreak of the Revolution drove him back to Holland. In 1789, with his accomplished wife, daughter, and son, he came to New York, where they at once became active in its musical life. In September, 1796, both father and son came to Boston, the senior as leader of the orchestra of the Hay-Market Theatre, and the junior as one of the violin players. They at once opened a "Musical Academy" at No. 62 Newbury Street (Washington Street), joined later by Mrs. von Hagen, pianist and teacher, who had lingered in New York. Here they also had their "Warranted Imported Piano Forte Ware House," and here, as P. A. von Hagen & Co., they began, late in 1797 or early in 1798, to publish music.

In May, 1798, Benjamin Crehore, the maker of 'cellos and basses, harpsichords and pianos, joined the firm, which became P. A. von Hagen Jun. & Co. In March, 1799, they moved to No. 55 Marlboro Street, as another section of Washington Street was then called; and again in May to No. 3 Cornhill. Here, as P. A. von Hagen & Co., the firm remained, maintaining until 1802 a separate "Piano Forte Ware House" at No. 4 old Massachusetts Bank, head of the Mall. On October 20, 1803, Peter von Hagen died at the age of forty-eight. His widow then removed to Common Street, and in 1806 to the corner of Short and Essex Streets. Among their publications are *Adams and Liberty*, *Adams and Washington*, *To Arms, Columbia*, and other patriotic songs of the day, besides the sentimental songs then in vogue and easy marches and dances.

Of the many patriotic songs of this troubled period, the most popular was *Hail! Columbia*, only rivaled by *Adams and Liberty*.

On Monday Evening, June 4, 1798, Mr. Barrett, the actor-manager, at his benefit at the Hay-Market Theatre sang Robert Treat Paine's song, *Adams and Liberty*, which had been published in Boston three days before. It was then advertised and afterward widely known as "The Boston Patriotic Song." Mr. Barrett

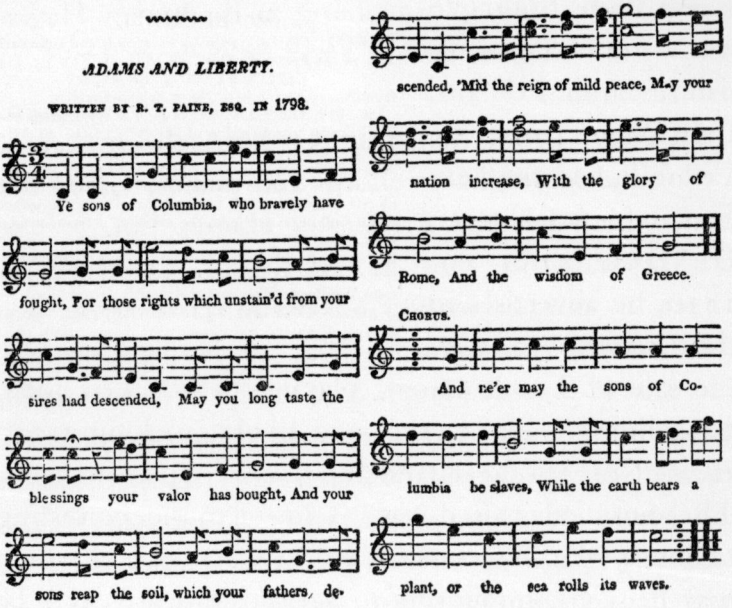

ADAMS AND LIBERTY.
WRITTEN BY R. T. PAINE, ESQ. IN 1798.

Ye sons of Columbia, who bravely have fought, For those rights which unstain'd from your sires had descended, May you long taste the blessings your valor has bought, And your sons reap the soil, which your fathers, descended, 'Mid the reign of mild peace, May your nation increase, With the glory of Rome, And the wisdom of Greece.

CHORUS.

And ne'er may the sons of Columbia be slaves, While the earth bears a plant, or the sea rolls its waves.

From "*Boston Musical Miscellany,*" 1815

also sang on this occasion "The Philadelphia Patriotic Song"—*Hail! Columbia;* and Mrs. Catherine Graupner sang, "accompanied on the Hautboy by Mr. Graupner." When President Adams attended the Hay-Market on June 5, 1799, John Hodgkinson, the eminent actor-vocalist and manager of the theatre, sang *Adams and Liberty*. This patriotic use of John Stafford

Smith's music became so popular that when Key's *Star-Spangled Banner* appeared in Baltimore in 1814 it was labelled "to be sung to the tune of *Adams and Liberty*."

In the *Independent Chronicle* of October 22, 1804, Pelham makes the following announcement:

William Blagrove was a son of Pelham's sister, Sarah Pelham. In 1808 he was at 61 Cornhill, and the next year at 3 School Street. On December 19, 1810, he advertises in the *Columbian Sentinel*

> W. PELHAM,
> RESPECTFULLY apprises his friends and customers of the Removal of his
> CIRCULATING LIBRARY,
> from No. 59, Cornhill, to No. 5, School-Street.
> W. P. having placed this branch of his business entirely under the direction of Mr. WILLIAM BLAGROVE, solicits a continuance of those favors he has been accustomed to receive during eight years past, the greater part of which time he has been constantly assisted by Mr. Blagrove, whose habitual attention to the wishes of his Customers precludes the necessity of recommendation.——A new Catalogue containing all the late additions, is in forwardness, and will shortly be published.
> ☞ BOOKS and STATIONARY for Sale, as as usual, at No. 59, CORNHILL.   Oct. 22.

the sale of Loo counters, playing cards, chess men, 50 gallons of black sand, and books, including 500 *Blair's Grave* in sheets, and 200 *Curfew*, a play in sheets. The music advertised was "A lot of music, consisting of Songs, Marches, Sonatas, etc. (a Catalogue of which may be seen), amounting to $400 or upwards, will be sold in sums of 10 dollars at 25 per cent discount, in sums of 50 to 100 dollars at 33 per cent discount from the retail price."

On April 27, 1811, the notice reproduced on the following page appeared in the *Columbian Sentinel*.

Samuel Hale Parker was born in Wolfboro, N. H., in 1781, the son of Matthew Stanley Gibson Parker. His uncles were Judge William Parker and Sheriff

John Parker of New Hampshire, and Bishop Samuel Parker of Boston. His brothers were Matthew Stanley Parker, cashier of the Suffolk Bank, and William Sewall Parker, a book-seller of Troy, N. Y.

After serving an apprenticeship to a bookbinder in 1802, Samuel H. Parker began as a

> **Union Circulating Library,**
> *No. 3, School-street.*
> SAMUEL H. PARKER, respectfully informs the patrons of this establishment and the public, that he has undertaken the future management of the business (Mr. BLAGROVE having relinquished it) and solicits continuance of the distinguished patronage it has hitherto experienced. Constant attention will be paid to the wishes of his customers, and large ADDITIONS are contemplated to be made during the summer, to the stock of circulating books.   apr 27
>
> **NOTICE.**
> W. BLAGROVE having relinquished the management of the business of the *Union Circulating Library*, respectfully calls upon those of his late customers from whom small arrearages are still due, for immediate settlement, as he is about closing his accounts with the Proprietor of the Establishment.
> ***Books which have been detained *over one month* must be returned; and all detained over 6 weeks *will be considered as purchased*, according to the conditions, unless immediately sent home.   apr 27

book-binder on Court Street, continuing that business until he took over the shop of William Blagrove in 1811. This shop was on the south side of School Street, three doors from Marlboro (now Washington Street). He continued at 3 School Street until he moved to 4 Cornhill, where he temporarily joined his interests with the book-sellers, Munroe & Francis, under the name *Munroe, Francis and Parker*, who so advertise in the *Columbian Sentinel* of September 13, 1815. The *Sentinel* of December 23, 1815, advertising the first concert of the Handel and Haydn Society states: "Tickets of admission may be obtained at the Bookstores of Munroe, Francis and Parker," and others, including "G. Graupner, Franklin Street." In 1816 Parker withdrew from the firm but remained at the corner of Water Street and Cornhill.

From time to time Parker advertises various book

publications, and October 18, 1817, he announces in the *Columbian Sentinel:* "Three Sacred Songs by Moore delightfully set to music by Oliver Shaw of Providence and sung by him at late Oratorios. *This World is all a Fleeting Show, Mary's Tears,* and *Thou art, O God! the Life and Light,* for sale at Parker's Circulating Library, 4 Cornhill." The same advertisement tells the public

View from Pemberton Hill in 1816, from the painting by Salmon

that he has "Just received a fresh supply of Vancouver's Iron Cement for mending glass and crockery."

The next year, 1818, his circulating library and music-store were moved to 12 Cornhill, one door south of the shop formerly occupied by Henry Knox. Here, in 1822, he advertises his "just published" edition of the Waverley Novels. Concerts of the period advertise "Tickets to be had at Mr. Parker's Music Store, No. 12 Cornhill, and at Mr. Graupner's Music Store, Franklin

Street." In 1825 Parker moved to 164 Washington Street, between Milk and Franklin, where he remained until fire destroyed the premises.

In the *Boston Transcript* of November 1, 1833, the following item appeared: "Fire. About half past three o'clock this morning fire was discovered in the cellar of building No. 164 Washington Street, owned by Mr. Benjamin Guild; insured for $7,500. The lower floor was occupied by Mr. Samuel H. Parker for a library and music-store, and John Price, optician. The second story was occupied by Mr. Benjamin Bradley, bookbinder, and Mr. Charles Bradlee, music-publisher, and the upper stories by Mr. Parker as a printing-office. Mr. Parker was insured for $10,000 in book-stock and $3,000 on printing-stock. A large portion of his library was destroyed, together with two valuable pianos, two printing-presses, and a large amount in sheet-stock. We are happy to learn, however, that none of the valuable stereotype plates of the Waverley Novels were lost, excepting one or two works which were in the process of being printed. The residue were stored in another place. Still his loss is severe, and just at the time he was upon the point of realizing the fruit of eight or ten years' hard labor in completing his edition of Scott's Novels, which would have been finished and come to market in December. Mr. Charles Bradlee lost a large portion of his sheet-music and plates."

In the *Transcript* of January 4, 1834, Parker advertises "Piano-fortes just received and for sale," at

[42]

10 School Street, but in the issue of April 5 "Sam'l H. Parker informs his friends that he has taken half of the store occupied by Mr. L. C. Bowles, 141 Washington Street, where he will renew the sale of *Music* and publishing the Waverley Novels which have been so unfortunately discontinued by the loss of his stock at the late fire," etc., etc. This location was three doors south of School Street. On July 1 he advertises that "He will have for sale all the Music published by Mr. C. Bradlee, with a constant supply of the new and fashionable Songs and Piano-forte pieces published at the South."

Parker's store became more and more a musical center, and on December 11, 1834, the *Transcript* states that "S. H. Parker has removed his music-store from 141 to 107 Washington Street." This shop, on the south corner of Williams Court, was shortly after occupied in part by the music-store of Oliver Ditson, who had some eight years earlier been in his employ.

At about the same time (January 20, 1835) the building into which Parker had moved was purchased by James A. Dickson who, as an actor, had come from England in 1796 to appear at the opening of the Hay-Market Theatre. Later he was manager of the Boston Theatre on Federal Street up to 1820, when he opened a "music saloon" on Market Street (now Cornhill), which had been recently made a thoroughfare. He was located there at the corner of Franklin Avenue for twenty years, but about 1835 Dickson turned his

[43]

activities more and more from selling music to marketing Day and Martin's blacking and Crosse and Blackwell's jam.

THE NINETEENTH CENTURY

State House and Common about 1820

IN 1800 Boston was a town of about 25,000 inhabitants, the earlier provincialism was passing, and evidences of interest in music for its own sake were becoming manifest. Music teachers had been increasing in numbers since the close of the Revolution, while growing prosperity and population gradually made it possible for shops for the sale of music and musical instruments to exist without the aid of other commodities. The change, however, was slow and the venturesome pioneers were as a rule musicians of standing in the community. Such was Gottlieb Graupner who, about 1800, began to publish music. This he engraved and printed with his own hands and sold at his "Musical Academy," No. 6 Franklin Street,

Gottlieb Graupner

[45]

where he also sold pianos and other instruments until February, 1820. According to *The Euterpiad*, his talented wife, Catherine, was "for many years the only female vocalist in Boston." She died in 1821, and Graupner in 1836.

Graupner was an all-round musician, at home on many instruments, and thirty years of age when, in 1797, he settled in Boston, where from 1798 until 1815 he was "the musical oracle." In 1810 the few instrumentalists of professional experience then living in Boston, together with a few amateurs, were organized by Graupner into The Philharmonic Society.* He had been oboist in Haydn's orchestra in London in 1791-1792, and soon his little orchestra practiced Haydn's symphonies for its own gratification and gave concerts of which that on Nov. 24, 1824, was the last.

These pioneers, von Hagen, Graupner, Lane, Prentiss, Keith, Hewitt, and Bradlee, helped to prepare the way for larger things, but the music-publisher in a national sense was yet to come, and there is little doubt that Graupner influenced his early career.

Oliver Ditson was of a family of Scotch descent living in Billerica, Massachusetts, in the last years of the seventeenth century. His grandfather, Samuel Ditson, was a Revolutionary soldier, living in Burlington, Massachusetts. Oliver's father, Joseph Ditson, born there in 1772, married in 1797, Lucy, the daughter of

---

*This name is also given as *Philharmonio* and *PhiloHarmonic*. A Philharmonic Society existed in 1799, according to a notice in the *Columbian Centinel* of April 6, 1799. Possibly it was the same society.

Solomon Pierce of Lexington, who was wounded on the morning of April 19, 1775, and later took part in the battle of Bennington.

Upon his marriage Joseph Ditson came to Boston. At that time property on the north side of Beacon Hill was being developed. Harrison Gray Otis had just finished his house, still standing on the corner of Lynde and Cambridge Streets. The Suffolk Registry of Deeds records that Joseph Ditson purchased of Appleton Prentiss a lot 40 x 70 feet on the newly laid out street between Russell and Irving Streets. Here he built a house in which he lived until 1810 when he moved to 74 Prince Street, near Copp's Hill, where on October 20, 1811, his fifth child, Oliver, was born. This house, now numbered 114, is on the west side of Prince Street.

The year 1811 was notable for the birth of Liszt and Thackeray, Charles Sumner and Harriet Beecher Stowe. The year before Chopin, Schumann, and Ole Bull were born. Of men destined to be significant in Boston's life, Emerson was then a lad of eight attending the public grammar school, Hawthorne was seven years old, Garrison six, Longfellow and Whittier four, and Oliver Wendell Holmes a baby of two. The year following, 1812, saw the outbreak of war with England as well as Napoleon's retreat from Moscow.

On Washington's Birthday, 1815, a musical jubilee was held in King's Chapel to celebrate the Peace of Ghent which concluded the war of 1812. Out of this originated, a few weeks later, The Handel and Haydn Society. One of the organizers and a member of the first board of trustees was Samuel H. Parker, then a member of Trinity choir. Another of the founders was G. Graupner, at whose Music Hall, 6 Franklin Street, the first meetings to organize the Society were held. It gave its first public concert in King's Chapel on Christmas Eve, 1815, and in 1818 gave the first complete performance of an oratorio in this country when it presented *The Messiah*. It was this society that in 1821 (dated 1822) published Lowell Mason's first collection of music after the publishers of Philadelphia and Boston had declined it. This was the very successful *Handel and Haydn Society Collection of Church Music*.

King's Chapel

It was in 1823 that young Oliver Ditson having finished his school life in the Eliot School on North Bennett Street, entered the employ of Colonel Parker, then at 12 Cornhill (Washington Street).

In 1824 the Public Garden was created on what had been an unsightly batch of mud on the west side of Charles Street. Boston was at this time a veritable garden city, and Summer Street with its overshadowing trees, lovely gardens and fine mansions, well merited its name.

In 1826 Lowell Mason settled in Boston, was next year made president and conductor of The Handel and Haydn Society, and thus began his notable public career not only as "The Father of American church music," but as the pioneer in inaugurating and developing the teaching of music in the public schools, formally introduced in 1838 as a regular branch of study in the Boston schools after two years of experimental work by Mason and his associate, Wm. C. Woodbridge.

In was in 1826 that young Ditson left S. H. Parker to apprentice himself to Isaac R. Butts, then printing *The North American Review*. Later he was with Alfred Mudge, and while there had charge of the printing for Colonel Parker, his former employer. At this time Ditson lived at 10 Province House Court, across the way from the prominent musician, Gottlieb Graupner, who then lived at No. 1. His son, John Henry Howard Graupner, and Oliver Ditson had been boys together, and the daughter of the former records the fact that her father carried for life a scar resulting from a wound given him by Oliver in some boyish rough and tumble play.

Mr. Ditson's innate fondness for music, his three years' training with Colonel Parker in the book and music business, his seven years' training as a printer, and possibly, also, his friendly relationship with the Graupner family, led him in 1835 to start in the music business at 107 Washington Street, just south of Williams Court.

He was at this time organist and choirmaster of the Bulfinch Street Church. The *Transcript* of October 13, 1834, advertises "SACRED CONCERT. The Singing Choir attached to Rev. Mr. Deane's Church in Bulfinch Street will perform a Concert of Sacred Music on Sunday Evening next, Oct. 19th at 6 1-2 o'clock. Tickets at 25 cents each, may be procured at S. H. Parker's Music Store, 141 Washington st; J. M. Smith's, Druggist, corner of School and Tremont sts.; and at the door on the evening of performance. Oliver Ditson, Sec'ry."

In December, 1834, as mentioned above, Colonel Parker moved from 141 Washington Street to No. 107. This brought him and his former employee together again under the same roof. Boston's population was then about 75,000. Postal rates were high, for it cost 18 3-4 cents to send a letter of a single sheet from Boston to New York. These were the days of the stage-coach, although they were soon to decline through the advent of railroads. It is recorded that in 1832 there were ninety-three stage lines running out of Boston.

What is, perhaps, the first mention of Oliver Ditson as a publisher appears in the *Saturday Evening Gazette* of June 6, 1835, which states in a reading notice: "Mr. Oliver Ditson has just published a new song entitled *There's not a Leaf within the Bower*. It was composed by F. Valentine, and arranged as a duet by Ch. Zeuner. It is for sale at Parker's Music Store." This was copyrighted June 5th by Oliver Ditson. The *Transcript* of June 20, 1835, says: "Ditson has in press *The City Guards Quick-step*, composed by Walch, and arranged as a duett for two flutes by Zeuner," and on July 9th advertises the same number as "Just published and for sale by S. H. Parker." This number was also copyrighted in the name of Oliver Ditson.

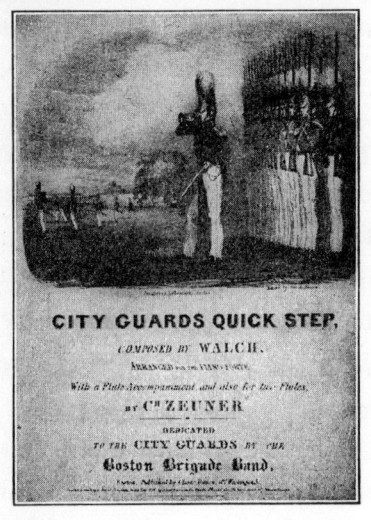

At this time Charles Zeuner was organist of Park Street Church and for the Handel and Haydn Society, and one of Boston's chief musicians. To him Mr. Ditson turned for editorial work, as the two publications just mentioned show, and in his first venturesome year of business the young publisher issued four or more songs by Zeuner—*The Songs of our Fathers* and *A Parting Song* (Mrs. Hemans), *Her last words of parting* (Thomas Moore), and *The lover's echo*, together with several of his instrumental numbers.

The *Gazette* of November 14, 1835, advertises a concert of the Handel and Haydn Society—"Tickets at Oliver Ditson's" and the *Transcript* of December

22, 1835, advertises a performance of *The Messiah* by the same society—"Tickets at Ditson's Music Store." The same paper in its issue of March 30, 1836, advertises the *Oratorio of David*, just published, as for sale at "Ditson's Music Store, 107 Washington Street," and that tickets for its approaching performance by the Handel and Haydn Society are to be had "at the Music Store of O. Ditson." Tickets for a concert by the Boston Academy were advertised in the *Boston Courier* of April 3d, "for sale at O. Ditson's."

On April 6th, the song, *My Heart's in the Highlands*, is advertised in the *Transcript* as for sale at "Ditson's Music Store." Apparently the younger man, by his energy and enthusiasm, was gaining precedence over his senior, who solved the problem by making Oliver his partner. The *Transcript* of April 5, 1836, contained the notice of copartnership.

The growing business of the new firm led them to seek better quarters, and in 1838 they had the good fortune to locate in the old gambrel-roofed building that since 1712 had stood on the site of the home of Anne Hutchinson, the first woman champion of intellectual freedom in America. In this old shop, at the corner of Washington and School Streets, books were sold continuously from 1828 to July, 1903. In 1837 the book-seller was William D. Ticknor, but it was in the days of James T. Fields that *The Old Corner Bookstore* became a gathering place for "the New England circle which compelled the world to acknowledge that there was an American literature." This location was then No. 135 Washington Street.

In 1840 Mr. Ditson married Miss Catherine Delano, a descendant of William Bradford, second Governor of Plymouth Colony. It was in this year that Boston was chosen as the terminus of the Cunard Line and the first regular trans-Atlantic steamer service began.

The Old Corner Bookstore

Railway connection with Worcester, Lowell, and Providence had been made in 1835, but with Albany not until 1841. There was not then a telegraph line in the world; Boston had a population of 93,383, New York 312,710, Philadelphia 93,665; Chicago was a frontier village of 4,479, while Kansas City, St. Paul, Minneapolis, and San Francisco had not been heard of.

Intersection of the Providence and Worcester railroads, 1838

It was just at this time that Henry Russell, the English ballad-singer, visited Boston, and his songs, *The Ship on Fire*, *The Maniac*, *The Gambler's Wife*, and others, were being sung with fervor in drawing-rooms; while, on the other hand, Margaret Fuller was holding her famous "Conversations" at Miss Peabody's rooms on West Street, and the Transcendentalists were making their Brook Farm experiment, with John S. Dwight as teacher of Music and Latin.

(No. 135)　　*West side of Washington Street in 1845*　　(No. 107)

[54]

In 1842 Mr. Ditson acquired the interests of his senior partner, as appears in the Dissolution of Copartnership notice, dated March 17, and printed in the *Transcript* the same day.

In need of larger quarters, Oliver Ditson moved in 1844 from the Old Corner Bookstore to a neighboring location

No. 115 to No. 107 Washington Street in 1845

at 115 Washington Street, four doors south of Williams Court. In the previous view of the west side of Washington Street the building at the right is No. 107, where Parker & Ditson were first located; the building at the left is No. 135, the Old Corner Bookstore location; while the sign to the right of the lamp post is that of Oliver Ditson at No. 115. In 1845 Mr. Ditson took into his employ a lad of fifteen, John C. Haynes, at the weekly stipend of $1.50. Eight years later, in 1853, the value of the young man was recognized by giving him an interest in the business, and on January 1, 1857, he was admitted to copartnership and the house name changed to Oliver Ditson & Co. In this year Mr. Ditson erected for his firm a building at 277, now 451 Washington Street.

It should be noted that Oliver Ditson's early friend and neighbor, John Henry Howard Graupner, had charge of his music-printing and engraving department from 1850, or earlier, until 1880. He was a good pianist and trained musician and son of the pioneer, Gottlieb Graupner, who taught him music-engraving.

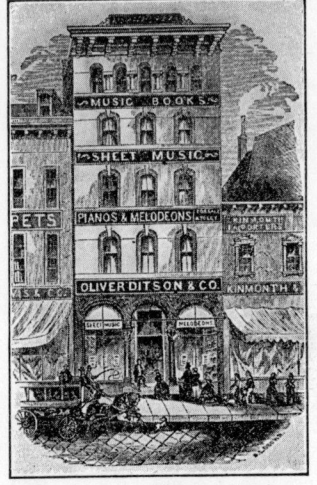

No. 277 Washington Street

∴

Probably the earliest American folio collection of glees and catches for two, three, and four or more voices was issued by Samuel H. Parker about 1823, the year when Oliver Ditson, as a boy, entered his employ. Its generous pages (10 x 14¼) contained such numbers as Danby's *Awake, Aeolian Lyre*, Mornington's *Here in cool grot*, Webbe's *When winds breathe soft*, and Mazzinghi's *Ye shepherds tell me*, together with others by Mozart, Shield, and Doctors Arne, Clarke, Calcott, and Stevenson. In his first venturesome years Oliver Ditson added a second series, and Parker & Ditson added a third series with the additional names of Bayley, Bishop, Horsley, and others.

Boston was then and for years after the chief center of choral activity in the country. It gave the first complete performance of Handel's *Messiah* in 1818, Haydn's *Creation* in 1819, Mendelssohn's *Elijah* in 1840, Rossini's *Stabat Mater* in 1843, Handel's *Samson* in 1845, *Judas Maccabeus* in 1847, Mendelssohn's *Hymn of Praise* in 1862, John K. Paine's *St. Peter* in 1847, Handel's *Joshua* in 1876, Bach's *Christmas Oratorio* in 1877, and Bach's *St. Matthew Passion* in 1879.

The first American edition of Haydn's *Creation* was issued by Oliver Ditson about 1845. Its large folio pages (10 x 15) must have been conspicuous when held up by a large chorus.

In addition to a long list of reprints of the standard oratorios, cantatas, and operas, from time to time new and important works were issued, for instance, the oratorio by George F. Bristow entitled, *Praise to God*, published in 1860; Eugene Thayer's *Festival Cantata*, 1872; J. C. D. Parker's choral ballad, *The Blind King*, 1883; John K. Paine's oratorio, *St. Peter*, 1874; Dudley Buck's *46th Psalm*; J. C. D. Parker's *Redemption Hymn*, 1877; Dr. Leopold Damrosch's oratorio, *Ruth and Naomi*, and other choral works. Important was the issue in 1869 of the first American edition of Bach's *Passion Music, according to St. Matthew*, with a new and masterly translation by John S. Dwight.

In 1853 Nathan Richardson, who had been a pupil of Alexander Dreyschock for nearly two years, published with the endorsement of William Mason, then in

Weimar, the *Modern School for Piano-Forte*, a technical work that included a series of large anatomical plates of the hand and forearm. Mr. Richardson published this purely technical work himself. It was but the forerunner of his enormously popular work, Richardson's *New Method for the Piano-Forte*. This work, published by Ditson in 1859, was a simplification of the earlier work, discarding its complexities and adapting the book to the needs of beginners; but the feature that gave it such extraordinary vogue was the abundant use of so-called "Amusements," tuneful, recreative music that gave the pupil a happy relief from the "Studies" and purely technical work. This was a new feature in instruction books for the piano, and brought a rich reward to both the author and the publisher.

In November, 1863, the dedication of the great concert-organ in Music Hall, Boston, gave marked impetus to the serious study of this instrument. This was followed soon after by the publication of another important pedagogic work—the first complete edition of *Rink's Organ School*, at that time the chief work of its type.

That New England was long the chief center for the publication of church and choral music has already been indicated. This lasted for over a century, from Josiah Flagg's *Collection of the Best Psalm Tunes*, Boston, 1764, through the era of Billings, Law, Holden, Holyoke, Belknap, Kimball, Morgan, Read, Swan, Shaw, and more than a dozen other native composers;

to the period of Lowell Mason, the master-spirit of a new group which included George J. Webb, Thomas Hastings, Isaac B. Woodbury, George F. Root, L. O. Emerson, William B. Bradbury, and others. A long list of these oblong anthem and hymn-books carried the imprint of Oliver Ditson & Co. Important were *The Ancient Lyre* by Charles Zeuner, 1836, taken over later by Mr. Ditson; *The Boston Glee Book* by Lowell Mason and George G. Webb, 1838, *Carmina Sacra* (Boston Collection of Church Music) issued by Lowell Mason in 1841 and later taken over. In the first ten years over 400,000 copies were sold of this outstanding book. In 1855 a revision was issued as *The New Carmina Sacra*. Under the sanction of the Musical Fund Society of Philadelphia, *Cantus Ecclesiae*, by H. W. Darley and J. C. B. Standbridge, was published in 1844 and later taken over by Ditson. Greatorex' *Church Music*, 1851, was also taken over, as was *The Shawm* by William B. Bradbury and George F. Root, issued in 1852.

The purchase of the catalog of Mason Brothers of New York brought in Lowell Mason's *The Hallelujah*, first issued in 1854, and *The Jubilee* of William B. Bradbury, of 1858, with many similar works. Mr. Ditson issued L. O. Emerson's *Harp of Judah* in 1863, and *Perkin's Anthem Book* in 1874. The books named are but typical examples of the many issued in this period.

This period of oblong board-bound books (6½ x 9¼) was followed by a group of larger oblong books (9¾ x 11¾). Typical examples were the earlier *Boston*

Academy's Collection of Choruses, 1836, and the *Academy Vocalist* of George F. Root, 1852, both taken over by Oliver Ditson & Co. Better remembered are Baumbach's *Sacred Quartets*, 1861, his *New Collection of Sacred Music*, 1871, and Dudley Buck's *Motette Collection*, 1864. Mr. Buck was then organist at the North Congregational Church of Hartford, Connecticut. His *Second Motette Collection* was issued in 1871.

The period of cumbersome choir-books was followed by the convenient octavo-sized issue of single numbers initiated in England by Novello & Co. The Ditson house was for some years their American agent. As early as 1869 the octavo list of English glees and part songs, and the most popular oratorio choruses, numbered about 150. In 1876 the present numbered series of octavo choral publications was initiated with the reprinting of English church music, together with the work of American composers, and since that date nearly 15,000 octavo numbers of sacred and secular choral music have been issued.

As already stated, the study of music in the public schools of America was officially inaugurated by Lowell Mason in Boston in 1838, after two years of experimental work. In the report of the Boston Academy of Music for July 1, 1839, this action of the Boston school-board in the face of a long and determined opposition was referred to as "The Magna Charta of musical education in this country." This teaching, at first confined to the grammar grades, was not systematically taught in the primary grades until 1864, nor in the high schools until Julius Eichberg's régime as supervisor, which began in 1869. In these early days the publishing of school-music books had not become a specialty and the field was open to the general music-publisher. Always alert for opportunities, Oliver Ditson was quick to enter this new field. Mason and Webb, as pioneers, had issued *The Juvenile Singing School* in 1837, and Lowell Mason issued *The Boston School Song Book* in 1841. Other cities cautiously followed the example of Boston, but over ten years elapsed before eight or nine important cities had introduced vocal music study. It took much longer than this before music had filtered into general educational thought; in fact, the methodical teaching of public school music was not firmly established until well after the Civil War. In 1856 Ditson issued the *Golden Wreath*, by L. O. Emerson, a book so popular that before 1872 over 300,000 copies had been sold. In 1860, *The Nightingale*, by W. O. & H. L. Perkins was published; followed by *The Golden Robin* of W. O. Perkins in 1868, *The Mocking Bird* in 1871, and *The Whip-poor-will* in 1876. In the period 1860-1880 a vast number of these and similar small, oblong school singing-books were circulated over the country.

The advertisement reproduced on the next page is taken from the issue of January 16, 1872, of *The Woman's Journal* of Boston, a weekly paper edited by Julia Ward Howe, Lucy Stone, Henry B. Blackwell,

Thomas Wentworth Higginson, and Mary A. Livermore, truly a notable and forward marching group. This compact advertisement throws a side-light on the Ditson choral publications sixty years ago, many of the works listed being the first American reprints to appear. The year 1872 was chorally notable through Boston's gigantic Peace Jubilee which may well represent the culmination of America's first choral period, 1815-1872, the fifty-seven years that began with the Musical Jubilee held in King's Chapel on Washington's Birthday, 1815, out of which sprang the Handel and Haydn Society. It was the close of the War of 1812 that led to the first event, and the close of the Franco-Prussian War in 1871 that led to the second.

OLIVER DITSON & CO.'S STANDARD MUSICAL WORKS.
CHEAP! UNEXCELLED!!

Beautiful Octavo Edition of Oratorios & Cantatas.

Creation	$.50	Stabat Mater	.45
Messiah	.50	Hymn of Praise	.50
Israel in Egypt	.50	Walpurgis Night	.75
Judas Maccabæus	.50	As the Hart pants (42 Ps)	.38
Samson	.75	Come let us sing (95 Ps)	.38
St. Paul	.75	Ninety-Eighth Psalm	.75
Elijah	1.00	Woman of Samaria	1.00
Athalia	1.00	Hear my Prayer	.38

Oratorio Choruses separate, 6 cts. each. 60 cts. per doz.

Beautiful Octavo Edition of Masses.

Beethoven's Mass in C	$.50	Mozart's 15th (Requiem) Mass	.50
Bordese's Mass in F	.75		
Concone's Mass in F	.60	Mozart's 2d, 7th and 9th Masses each	.75
Farmer's Mass in B flat	.75	Mercadante's Mass, 3 voices	.75
Gounod's Mass Solennelle	.75	Niedermayer's Mass in D	1.25
Haydn's 3d Mass	.45		
Haydn's 1st, 2d, 3d, 4th, 7th and 8th Masses, each	.75	Rossini's Messe Solennelle	1.60
		Weber's Mass in G	.50
Haydn's 16th Mass	1.00	Weber's Mass in E flat	.75
De Monti's Mass	.75	Southard's Mass in F	.83
Mozart's 1st Mass	.60	" short Mass in D	.38
Mozart's 12th Mass	.45		

Complete Operas, Full Vocal Score.
INCLUDING RECITATIVES, $1.00 EACH.

FAUST, FIDELIO, MARTHA, TRAVIATA, SOMNAMBULA, DON GIOVANNI, MARRIAGE of FIGARO, NORMA, ERNANI, PRECIOSA, TROVATORE, FRA DIAVOLO, LUCRETIA BORGIA, LUCIA.

*** The above can be had of any Music Dealers, or the Publishers. Sent, post-paid, on receipt of price.

Oliver Ditson & Co., BOSTON. | C. H. Ditson & Co., 711 BROADWAY, N. Y.
Mar. 16.

∴

The year 1841 is notable in that Beethoven's symphonies, the *First* and *Fifth*, were then first heard in Boston. They were performed by the Academy of Music Orchestra, of from twenty-five to forty players, which for seven winters gave a series of six to eight concerts, the last in the spring of 1847. It was at one of its concerts, March 7, 1846, that Wm. Mason, then seventeen, made his first appearance as a pianist.

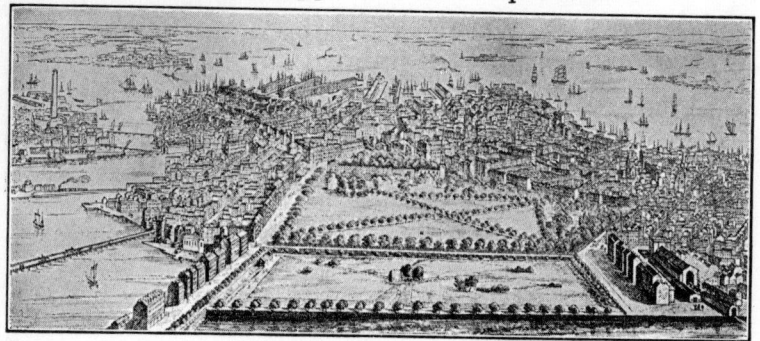

Bird's-eye view of the Public Garden and Common, about 1850

These concerts were succeeded by those of the Musical Fund Society, which for eight seasons gave orchestral concerts in the old Tremont Temple, its last concert being given April, 1855, in the then new Boston Music Hall.

A still better organization, rich in soloists, was the Germania Orchestra, which from 1848 to 1854, travelled, but gave from eighty to ninety of its concerts in Boston, where they made their first appearance April 14, 1849, and gave twenty-two concerts in six weeks. This little orchestra of twenty-three was sometimes doubled by the addition of local musicians. The precision, delicacy and beauty of their performances of the best music left a lasting influence.

It was this orchestra that brought Carl Zerrahn to Boston as its first flute. In 1854 he became conductor of the Handel and Haydn Society, and in 1855 he organized the Philharmonic Orchestra, which gave regular concerts until 1863. In 1865 Zerrahn was made conductor of the orchestra of the Harvard Musical Association, which for seventeen years maintained symphony concerts of a high standard.

Carl Zerrahn

In the musical life of America for many years no single man wielded so potent an influence for musical righteousness as Theodore Thomas. He had a whole-souled belief in the power of good music and devoted his life to making it known. The frequent visits of his orchestra to Boston overshadowed the less disciplined and imperfect local body, sharpened musical perception, and wakened concert-goers to the need of an orchestra of like technical refinement and masterly leadership. This need was generously met by Mr. Henry Lee Higginson when he founded the Boston Symphony

Henry Lee Higginson

[64]

Orchestra, which gave its first concert under Georg Henschel, October 22, 1881, and under Gericke, Nikisch, and their successors, has developed into the present unique organization.

It was the Harvard Musical Association, organized in 1837 by John S. Dwight, Henry K. Oliver, William Wetmore Story, Christopher P. Cranch, and others, that by its regular *soirées* from 1844 to 1850 initiated Boston into the beauties of chamber music. Stimulated by these affairs the Mendelssohn Quintette Club was organized with Thomas Ryan as its leading spirit. It was the first chamber music organization of its type in the country and gave its first concert December 14, 1849. For nearly fifty years this club travelled over the United States, making classical music known to multitudes for the first time.

It was also the moral backing of the Harvard Musical Association that led John S. Dwight to establish *Dwight's Journal of Music* in 1852. For six years he was editor, publisher, and proprietor, when, in 1858, the magazine was taken over by Oliver Ditson & Co., who published it until the end of 1878, Mr. Dwight continuing as editor. It was carried on by other publishers until 1881, when it

John S. Dwight

ceased to exist. Its first number was issued April 10, 1852; its last, September 3, 1881. This pioneer magazine was a notable factor in moulding musical opinion and its pages are the history of music in the United States during the twenty-nine years of its existence.

Giulia Grisi

Jenny Lind in 1850

While foreign artists had come and gone, the year 1850 ushered in a notable galaxy, beginning with Jenny Lind and her memorable concerts, the lovely Sontag, and the great Alboni, followed by Patti, Grisi and Mario, Adelaide Phillips, Brignoli, Parepa Rosa, and a host of lesser singers.

It was in February, 1853, that Jenny Lind was married to Otto Goldschmidt, her accompanist, in the house in quaint Louisburg Square, at the left in the illustration. It stands

Urso at 11

Teresa Carreño, Anna Mehlig, Rubinstein, von Bülow, Essipoff, and others.

Of violinists, Vieuxtemps, Ole Bull, Sivori, and Camilla Urso, "the girl violinist," were early comers, followed

Carreño at 10

almost on the site of the apple orchard of Boston's first inhabitant.

Of pianists, Thalberg, who came in 1857, was perhaps the first of great rank. The early sixties brought home from Europe, Gottschalk; then came the war and a lull, followed by the girl wonder,

Great Organ in Music Hall

by Wieniawski, Wilhelmj, Remenyi, Sauret, and others.

Organ playing in the country was given a stimulus when the great organ in Boston Music Hall was opened November 2, 1863. This large instrument was the first thorough concert organ in the country. A notable group of organists, B. J. Lang, John K. Paine, Eugene Thayer, S. P. Tuckerman, John H. Wilcox, and George W. Morgan were the first to play upon it.

The sensational event of 1869 was the monster Peace Jubilee, organized by P. S. Gilmore; Carl Zerrahn was general director; John K. Paine and Dudley Buck conducted compositions of their own; Julius Eichberg wrote for the occasion his *To Thee, O Country*, now sung in the schools everywhere, and Ole Bull and Carl Rosa played in the big orchestra, while Parepa Rosa and Adelaide Phillips were the chief singers. A festival building large enough to seat thirty thousand persons was erected near the site of the present Copley Plaza Hotel; the orchestra numbered one thousand, and the chorus ten thousand. The sensitive John S. Dwight refused to endorse the Jubilee in his *Journal of Music* and fled to Nahant to escape the cannons, anvils, bells, big organ, eighty-four trombones, eighty-three tubas, as many cornets, and

B. J. Lang

Julius Eichberg

seventy-five drums, which with three hundred and thirty strings and one hundred and nineteen wood-wind, made "an ensemble of fearful and wonderful sonority."

The ambitious Gilmore found another opportunity at the close of the Franco-Prussian War when he organized on a still larger scale the International Peace Jubilee of June, 1872. This time the auditorium seated fifty thousand; the chorus, collected from over the country as far west as Omaha, numbered twenty thousand and the orchestra two thousand. Johann Strauss and Franz Abt led their own compositions. Mme. Rudersdorff was the chief singer, and famous bands from London, Dublin, Paris, Berlin, Washington, and New York were features. Though the first Jubilee cost $283,000, it left a balance of nearly $10,000 in the treasury;

Hermine Rudersdorff

the second "colossal musical picnic" left a deficit of $100,000 to be made up by the guarantors, among them Oliver Ditson.

In contrast to these monster festivals were the smaller and musically more important triennial festivals of the Handel and Haydn Society. It was at the festival of 1871 that about half of Bach's *St. Matthew Passion Music* was given for the first time in America, still more was given in 1874, and on Good Friday, 1879, the entire work had a notable performance in a two-session concert.

How recent serious composition in the larger forms is in America, is indicated by the fact that our pioneer symphonist, John K. Paine, left us as recently as 1906. It was in the year of MacDowell's birth, 1861, that he returned to Cambridge from study in Germany. His first symphony was played in 1876, and when those in charge of the Centennial Exposition sought the two native composers of greatest prominence to write the music for the opening ceremonies they selected John K. Paine and Dudley Buck.

John K. Paine

Since then a notable group have enriched American composition with symphonies, orchestral works, chamber music and choral works, while a host have written in small forms; but to speak of men until recently with us or of the many now active in creative work, interpretation and education, is beyond the scope of this brief sketch of a bygone day.

Dudley Buck

SEVENTY YEARS MORE

In 1860, Mr. Ditson established in Cincinnati, Mr. John Church, a young man who had been with him from boyhood. The business successfully launched was in 1871 sold to Mr. Church, and is now well known as the John Church Company.

In 1864, two young men, Mr. P. J. Healy and Mr. George W. Lyon, were established in Chicago by the capital of Oliver Ditson & Co., under the now honored name of Lyon & Healy.

John Church

On March 4, 1867, the firm purchased the music plates, stock and good-will of Firth, Son & Co. of New York City. This led at once to the establishment of a branch house in the metropolis, under the management of Oliver Ditson's eldest son, Charles, with the firm name of Chas. H. Ditson & Co.

P. J. Healy

After remaining a few months at 563 Broadway,

where Firth, Son & Co. had been located, more spacious quarters were taken at 711 Broadway. The purchase by the parent house of the music catalog and business of Wm. Hall & Son of New York, in 1875, and of J. L. Peters of New York, in 1877, necessitated the taking of more spacious quarters, in 1878, at 843 Broadway.

In 1883, the property at the southwest corner of Broadway and Eighteenth Street was purchased and the Ditson Building erected. Here at 867 Broadway the firm remained until the constant uptown trend of retail trade led to the erection of a new Ditson Building at 8-10-12 East 34th Street. Into these handsome quarters the firm moved in 1907, just forty years after its establishment.

∴

In 1875, the purchase of the catalog of Lee & Walker of Philadelphia, led to the opening of a branch house in that city under the management of another son, James Edward Ditson, under the firm name of J. E. Ditson & Co.

In 1879, the stock and music plates of G. André & Co. of Philadelphia, were purchased.

In 1881, the uptown trend of business led to the removal from 922 to 1228 Chestnut Street. In the same year occurred the death of Mr. J. E. Ditson.

8-12 East 34th Street

In 1890, the entire catalog, stock and music plates of F. A. North & Co. of Philadelphia, were purchased.

In 1910, changed conditions of business led to the discontinuance of the Philadelphia branch house.

∴

In 1877, the purchase of the catalog and good-will of G. D. Russell & Co. of Boston, and the constantly expanding business of the parent Boston house compelled the taking of the adjoining store at No. 449 Washington Street, which had been erected expressly as an addition to No. 451.

449-451 *Washington Street*

With the issue of December 21, 1878, Oliver Ditson & Co. ceased to publish *Dwight's Journal of Music* and established the *Monthly Musical Record*, which in 1898 was succeeded by the *Musical Record*, a high-class magazine under the brilliant editorship of Philip Hale.

In October, 1898, the issue was begun of a pocket-size monthly magazine to bulletin the publications of the house, under the name *Music Review*.

In January, 1901, this magazine was combined with the *Musical Record* under the name *Musical Record & Review*, with Thomas Tapper as editor. After more than two years' issue in its enlarged form another combination was made by the purchase from the Hatch Music Company of Philadelphia of the *Musician*. The smaller magazine was dropped and the new magazine in its present form issued under Mr. Tapper's editorship from November, 1903, to August, 1907, when he was succeeded by Mr. W. J. Baltzell, who conducted the magazine until December 31, 1918. Through its purchase by a New York magazine publisher, the issue of January, 1919, appeared in the metropolis under new editorship and management. In May, 1922, the magazine passed into the hands of Mr. Paul Kempf, its present owner and editor.

As already indicated, the period 1860-1890 was a time of great expansion. Not only was the constant output of new publications large, but the purchase of over fifty other catalogs increased the bulk of the already big Ditson catalog. As some of these publishers were the successors of still earlier houses, by their absorption into the Ditson catalog the house became directly linked to the early publishers of New York, Philadelphia, and Baltimore. As a matter of record the more important of these publishing houses are listed:

Boston	*New York*
L. W. Blanchard	J. F. Atwill
Charles Bradlee	Brentano Bros.
Charles H. Keith	A. Cortada & Co.
A. & J. P. Ordway	Firth, Son & Co.
J. F. Perry & Co.	William Hall & Son
Carl Prüfer	Mason Brothers
G. D. Russell & Co.	Martens Bros.
Russell Bros.	J. L. Peters
E. H. Wade	Spear & Denhoff

Philadelphia
G. André & Co.
A. Fiot
Lee & Walker
F. A. North & Co.
W. F. Shaw
C. W. A. Trumpler
Septimus Winner

Baltimore
Henry McCaffrey
Miller & Beacham

Buffalo
A. Rottenbach
J. H. Wahle & Son

Louisville
H. Knoefel

Cincinnati
F. W. Helmick
Newhall & Evans Music Co.
Truax & Baldwin

San Francisco
Matthias Gray

The printed Ditson catalogs of 1890, which culminated the period of expansion, list 100,000 titles, classified as follows: Vocal music, 45,000; Octavo music, 4,000; Instrumental music, 48,000; Books, 3,000.

Forty years later the printed Ditson catalogs of 1930 included, in round numbers, 20,000 titles. In considering this deflation it should be remembered that the catalogs of 1890 frankly stated that many of the titles were listed for completeness sake, were no longer active, and some of the numbers could not be supplied; moreover, the bulk of this great catalog included the accretions due to the purchase of many other catalogs. Fashions in music change, and after a few initial years of activity many numbers drop into desuetude. The catalogs of 1930 are therefore made up chiefly of new and active material, for the silent process of elimination of inactive publications is as continuous as the constant adding of new numbers. Moreover, the period 1897-

1920 was one of rehabilitation, when thousands of plates were re-engraved and old editions were superceded or discarded. The 20,000 titles listed in the Ditson catalogs of 1930 may be classified as follows: Vocal music, 3,450; Octavo, choir, and choral music, 6,800; Instrumental music, 7,180; and Books, 2,570.

On December 21, 1888, Oliver Ditson passed away at the ripe age of seventy-seven. He had been not only a great music-publisher, but for twenty years President of the Continental Bank, director in various institutions, a constant though unostentatious promotor of good works in others, and the quiet helper of many a struggling musician. On Sunday afternoon, December 23, he was buried from Trinity Church, the Rev. Phillips Brooks officiating. Mr. J. C. D. Parker, the son of his early employer, presided at the organ. The surviving partners, John C. Haynes, Charles H. Ditson, and the executors of Oliver Ditson's estate then organized the corporation, Oliver Ditson Company, with Mr. Haynes as President.

Oliver Ditson

In 1891, larger quarters being needed, the extensive

[76]

property at 453-463 Washington Street, known as the Dexter Building, was leased and occupied until 1901.

Mr. Charles H. Ditson having erected a modern ten-story building at 451 Washington Street, on the site of the five-story building erected by his father in 1857 for Oliver Ditson & Co., the business was in 1901 moved into it. Changing conditions

453-463 *Washington Street*

and the necessity of still larger quarters caused the removal on January 25, 1904, to the new building constructed for its special needs at 150 Tremont Street, facing Boston Common. Upon the death May 3, 1907, of Mr. John C. Haynes, after sixty-two years' connection with the house, the Presidency of the corporation and the direction of

451 ↑ *Washington St.*

John C. Haynes

[77]

its great interests devolved naturally and fittingly upon the son of the founder, Mr. Charles Healy Ditson.

The eight-story building at 150 Tremont Street, proving too cramped, Mr. Ditson erected a larger and thoroughly modern ten-story building at 178-179 Tremont

150 Tremont Street

178-179 Tremont Street

Street, into which the business was moved in September, 1917.

On May 14, 1929, Mr. Charles H. Ditson passed on at the ripe age of eighty-four. He had been active in music-publishing for sixty-four years and a resident of New York City for sixty-two years, first as head of Chas. H. Ditson & Co. from its inception, and President of the Oliver Ditson Company for twenty-two years. Of unremitting activity, unostentatious generosity,

[78]

Charles Healy Ditson

ever seeking to avoid publicity, it was not disclosed until his will had been made public that he had bequeathed $800,000 to the cause of music education, giving $100,000 each to Harvard, Yale, Princeton, and Columbia Universities, and a similar sum to the New England Conservatory of Music and other institutions.

In May, 1929, Mr. H. Hobart Porter of New York City succeeded to the presidency, and on February 2, 1931, the publishing business and the great Ditson catalog were purchased by the Theodore Presser Company of Philadelphia, which in 1930 had purchased the John Church Company of Cincinnati, a house established in 1860 by Oliver Ditson. Rooted in Boston, linked to its traditions and nationally known as a Boston institution, the new directors wisely voted to preserve the autonomy of the Ditson Company and to continue unchanged its established publishing policy and business methods.

Between the death of Oliver Ditson in 1888 and January 1, 1897, the publishing policy of the house continued along its accustomed lines, but realizing the need for a more clearly-defined and more progressive policy, Mr. John C. Haynes, then President, brought to this task a young man who combined business experience with trained musicianship and high ideals. His task was to raise the level and improve the quality of the publications, and to eliminate that which was below standard. Not only was the output greatly reduced, out-dated publications withdrawn from the catalog, and standard works edited and re-engraved, but a notable series of educational works was initiated. Thus, without revolution but by a steady and gradual evolution, the catalog was remade and a high standard of publication firmly established. In 1897 the important series of pedagogic books, *The Music Students Library*, was begun and now includes over forty textbooks.

The most notable of these various series of books is *The Musicians Library*, begun in 1903. This unique series of nearly one hundred volumes was planned to include the masterpieces of song and piano music in volumes beautiful in engraving, typography, illustration, printing, and binding, each book edited by a man of the highest authority in America or Europe. This truly notable series was made possible by the enthusiastic and generous support of Mr. Charles H. Ditson. In 1912 the upspringing of class-teaching of the violin and other instruments in our public schools gave rise to the pioneer series of *Mitchell's Class Methods*. In 1915 a series of song-anthologies was begun, edited, not by critics, but by such famous singers as Calvé,

Culp, Farrar, Gerhardt, Gluck, and Sembrich from their own repertoire.

In 1918 the movement for granting credit to high-school students for the outside study of music made necessary a standard text that combined with piano study the correlative studies that make for musicianship. Under the joint editorship of three educators of national reputation *The Music Students Piano Course* was issued in twenty books.

To the rapid expansion of the school-orchestra movement is due the *Philharmonic Orchestra Series*, the pioneer series to provide the conductor with a complete score for each number. This series, begun in 1921, now contains over fifty numbers of genuine musical worth.

In 1924 the publication of the first correlated series of books on music appreciation was begun under the title, *A Study Course in Music Understanding*. Although these five books by such able specialists as Gehrkens, Goetschius, Hamilton, Kelley, and Mason were written to fit the needs of the general reader and the National Federation of Music Clubs, they are widely used as text-books.

The demand for fully-scored band-music of a high type led in 1926 to the *Symphonic Band Series*. An important educational series that has no duplicate is the *Analytic Symphony Series*, begun in 1927 under the scholarly editorship of Dr. Percy Goetschius. Nearly forty of the great symphonies have already been issued in meticulously edited two-hand piano scores with analytical and critical notes on the structure, orchestration, and place of the work in the composer's creative development. A series of compact, low-priced original books of distinct educational value was begun in 1927 as *The Pocket Music Student*. Fifteen of these books have already been issued. Enough has been said to indicate the distinctly educational character of the Ditson publishing policy, which has in no way been changed by the new ownership.

Tremont Street from West Street to Boylston Street, March, 1918

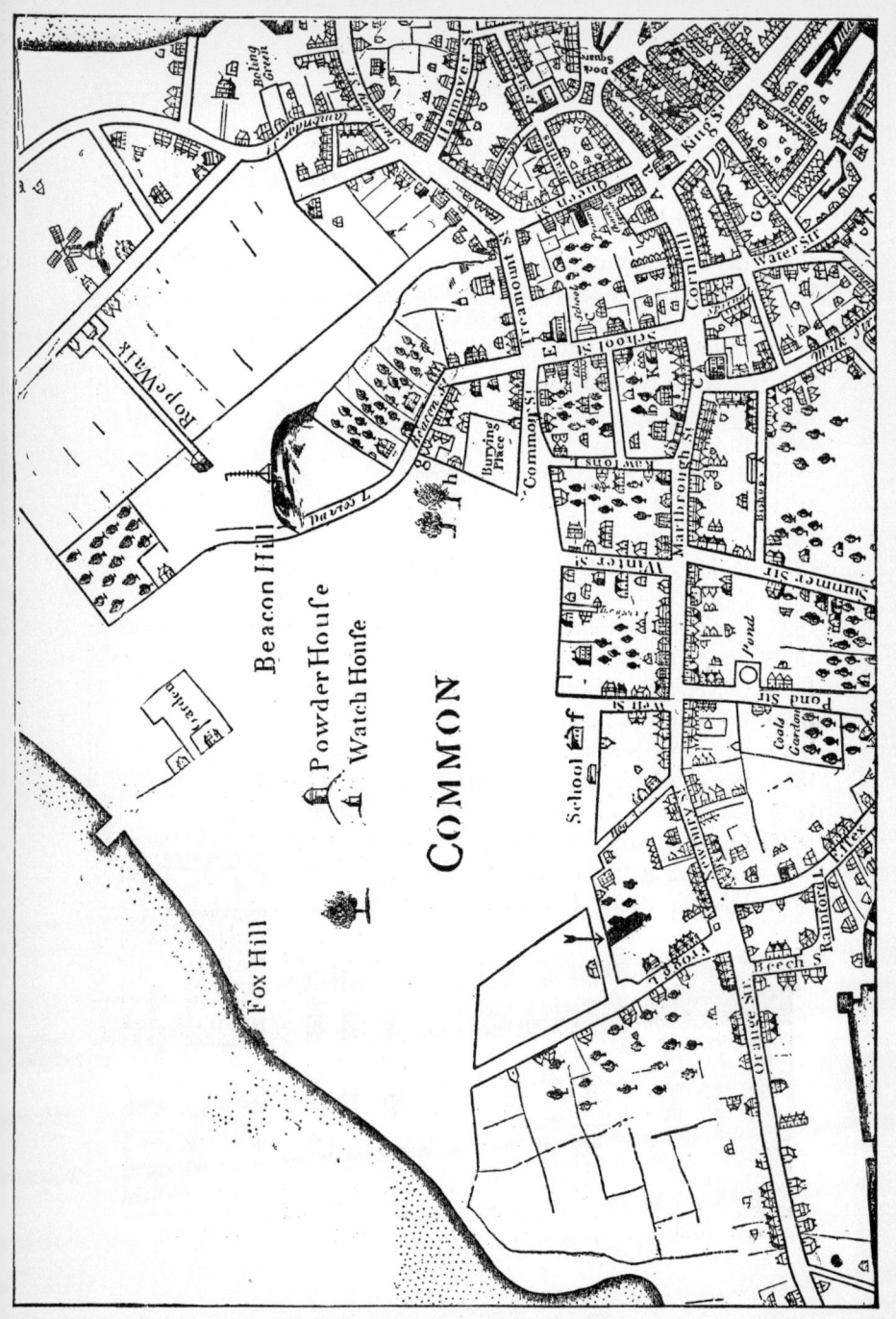

From Bonner's Map of Boston, 1722
(The arrow points to the site of the Hay-Market Theatre)

CHRONOLOGY OF
THE OLIVER DITSON COMPANY

1783   Ebenezer Battelle opens the Boston Book-Store at 8 State Street.
1785   Benjamin Guild purchases Battelle's music and circulating library.
1786   Guild moves to 59 Cornhill (Washington Street).
1792   Guild dies and William Pinson Blake continues the business.
1796   William Pelham succeeds Blake at 59 Cornhill.
1804   William Blagrove takes Pelham's business at 5 School Street.
1808   Blagrove moves to 61 Cornhill (Washington Street).
1809   Blagrove moves to 3 School Street.
1811   Samuel H. Parker succeeds Blagrove at 3 School Street.
1811   Oliver Ditson born in Boston on October 20.
1815   Parker moves to 4 Cornhill (Washington Street).
1818   Parker moves to 12 Cornhill (Washington Street).
1823   Oliver Ditson enters the employ of Colonel S. H. Parker.
1825   Parker moves to 164 Washington Street.
1826   Oliver Ditson becomes an apprentice to Isaac R. Butts.
1833   Fire destroys Parker's store, November 1.
1834   Parker reopens in January at 10 School Street.
1834   Parker moves in April to 141 Washington Street.
1834   Parker moves in December to 107 Washington Street.
1835   Oliver Ditson begins to publish and copyright music at 107 Washington Street.
1836   Firm of Parker & Ditson formed on April 5.

1835–1838    1838–1844 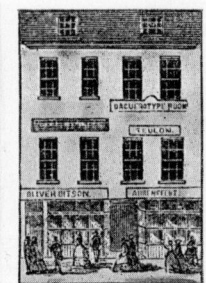   1844–1857    1857–1877

1838 Parker & Ditson move to 135 Washington Street.
1842 Oliver Ditson acquires the interests of Samuel H. Parker.
1844 Oliver Ditson moves to 115 Washington Street.
1845 John C. Haynes enters the employ of Oliver Ditson.
1857 Oliver Ditson & Co. formed by admitting John C. Haynes.
1857 Mr. Ditson erects building at 277 (now 451) Washington Street.
1858 Oliver Ditson & Co. take over *Dwight's Journal of Music*.
1860 Mr. Ditson establishes John Church in Cincinnati.
1864 Mr. Ditson establishes Lyon & Healy in Chicago.
1867 Chas. H. Ditson & Co. established in New York.
1875 J. E. Ditson & Co. established in Philadelphia.
1877 Store at 449 Washington Street taken as an addition to No. 451.
1881 Death of James Edward Ditson.
1888 Death of Oliver Ditson, December 21.
1889 Oliver Ditson Company incorporated, John C. Haynes, Pres.
1891 Removal to 453–463 Washington Street.
1901 Removal to new ten-story building at 451 Washington Street.
1904 Removal to new and larger building at 150 Tremont Street.
1907 Death of John C. Haynes.
1907 Charles H. Ditson, President.
1917 Removal to new building at 178–179 Tremont Street.
1929 Death of Charles H. Ditson.
1929 H. Hobart Porter, President.
1931 Purchase by Theodore Presser Company.
1931 Removal to 359 Boylston St.

1877–1891    1891–1901    1901–1904    1904–1917

[85]

THE 19ᵀᴴ CENTURY & AFTER

PHILADELPHIA PUBLISHERS

Of the eighteenth century publishers who carried on into the nineteenth, John Aitken lasted a few years at 76 North Second Street, and Ralph Shaw at 13 South Fourth Street is listed in the directory of 1803 and then disappears. The pioneer Benjamin Carr seems to have soon given up his music-shop and confined his activities to teaching, conducting, organ-playing, and composition. As Carr & Schetky he issued from time to time a *Musical Journal* consisting of music by Braham, Cimarosa, Hook, Pleyel, Shield, Carr himself, and others. For years Carr was the chief figure in Philadelphia's musical life and was one of the founders of the Musical Fund Society in 1820, and one of the choral conductors at its first concert, April 24, 1821. He conducted the first performances in Philadelphia of portions of the *Messiah* and the *Creation*. Held in the highest esteem he passed on May 24, 1831, at the age of sixty-two.

The only eighteenth century Philadelphia publisher linked to the present day is George Willig. Born in 1764, he settled in Philadelphia about 1793 and opened his Musical Magazine at 163 North Third Street in November, 1794. In 1800 he was located at 185 High Street; from 1805 to 1816 he was at 12, then at 24

South Fourth Street; and from 1817 he was at 171 Chestnut Street, and in 1854 at 518 Chestnut Street, until his catalog was taken over by Lee & Walker in 1856. In 1845 Julius Walker conducted a "library" at 120 Walnut Street, and in that year took into partnership George W. Lee and added music to his stock of books. Soon music predominated and in 1849, at Chestnut Street below Seventh Street, they added musical instruments to their stock and published music. In 1856 the firm, which now included William W. Walker, took over the catalog of Philadelphia's oldest music-publisher, George Willig, and continued at shifting Chestnut Street addresses until 1875 when the Lee & Walker catalog was purchased by Oliver Ditson & Co. of Boston. By this purchase the Philadelphia Willig of 1793 was linked to the successor of the Battelle of Boston of 1783. This led to the establishment in 1875 of J. E. Ditson & Co. at the old Lee & Walker address, 922 Chestnut Street. In 1881 the new house moved to 1228 Chestnut Street and in 1905 to No. 1632, where it remained until 1910 when this branch of the Boston house was discontinued.

Of the other Philadelphia publishers in the first half of the nineteenth century George E. Blake was important. Beginning late in 1803, or early in 1804, at 1 South Third Street, from 1814 to 1840 he was located at 13 South Fifth Street, going thence to 25 South Fifth Street, where he remained until 1871. Other publishers of this period were Allyn Bacon who, as A. Bacon at 11 South Fourth Street in 1814, as Allyn Bacon & Co., again as A. Bacon, and in 1819 as Bacon & Hart, continued at the same address. In 1833 the firm became Bacon, Weygand & Co., and soon after they were absorbed by the older firm of Klemm & Bro. at 273 Market Street. It was in October, 1818, that J. G. Klemm & Bro. began as "instrument and music-sellers" at 1 North Fourth Street. At various addresses this firm was active as dealers and publishers until 1880.

Of mid-century publishers are G. André & Co. of 19 South Ninth Street, then at 1104 Chestnut Street and at No. 1228 from 1851 until 1879, when the catalog was bought by Oliver Ditson & Co. Francis A. North was a member of this firm until late in 1870, or early in 1871, when he established his own business at 654 North Eleventh Street. As F. A. North & Co. at 1026 Chestnut Street he absorbed, in 1872, the music and publishing business of Charles W. A. Trumpler, a firm that started in 1865 at 632 Chestnut Street, going later to No. 926. North & Co. continued until 1890 at 1308 Chestnut Street, when the combined North and Trumpler catalogs were purchased by Oliver Ditson & Co.

Augustus Fiot of 264 High Street in 1834 combined with Leopold Meignen, the musician, in 1835 as Fiot, Meignen & Co. at 264 High Street. In 1837 they moved to 217 Chestnut Street, but from 1843 to 1855 Fiot conducted the business alone at 196 Chestnut Street. He was succeeded in 1855 by J. E. Gould

& Co. at 164 Chestnut Street, Mr. John E. Gould having been a music-publisher in New York at 297 Broadway (1851-1853). They, in turn, were followed late in 1856, or early in 1857, by James M. Beck and Dennis Lawton as Beck & Lawton. This firm lasted until 1863, when it became J. W. Lawton & Co. at 19 South Eighth Street and then disappeared. Later the Fiot catalog was purchased by Oliver Ditson & Co. W. H. Boner & Co. were at 1102, 1314, and 1419 Chestnut Street for the thirty-five years, 1865-1900.

Mention should be made of a modest man whose unusual name, Septimus Winner, became widely known as the publisher of vocal numbers issued over his pen-name, Alice Hawthorne. Three of these: *Listen to the Mocking Bird*, *Whispering Hope*, and *What is Home without a Mother?* had an enormous circulation; and his series of compact, inexpensive, and popular methods for all the instruments, known as Winner's *Eureka Methods*, have given millions of beginners their first introduction to instrumental music. With his brother Joseph Winner he opened a music-shop at 348 North Third Street in 1845. In 1855 it became Winner & Shuster at 110 North Eighth Street, but in a few years Mr. Winner was again sole proprietor until in 1871, with his son J. Gibson Winner as partner, the firm name became Septimus Winner & Son. In 1885 they were at 545 North Eighth Street and in 1887, or early in 1888, the catalog was purchased by Oliver Ditson & Co. and the Winner firm ceased to exist.

This brief summary clearly indicates the precariousness of music-publishing of the miscellaneous type — a ceaseless issue of music of the style in vogue at the hour, but without a clearly outlined policy or a definite focal point. In the post-bellum period when war-songs were out of date and New York was becoming more and more the publishing center, there was obviously a lull in music-publishing in Philadelphia, and little did a tall, lank boy in a Pittsburgh music-store dream that some day he would own the largest music establishment in the Quaker city and that his name would be known in every city, town, and hamlet where music is taught. His musical bent led the eager youth in 1872 to the New England Conservatory of Music in Boston and in 1878 to the Leipzig Conservatory, in those days the Mecca of all ambitious students. Young Presser on his return taught music in several Ohio colleges and later at Hollins Institute in Virginia.

It was in 1883 at Lynchburg, Va., that Theodore Presser with $250 in cash and an intangible million in energy, pluck, and ambition started *The Etude*. In 1876 he had been the leader in founding the Music Teachers National Association and felt that if it was to expand it must have a

Theodore Presser

journal; he also saw the great need of music-teachers everywhere for plain, practical guidance and helpful stimulus. So in October, 1883, he left Lynchburg for Philadelphia and in June, 1884, opened an office at 1004 Walnut Street. In those days of struggle as editor, owner, and publisher of this paper he was buoyed up by the hope that he would some day attain a monthly circulation of 5,000 copies — expecting to return to teaching when the magazine was established. In order to carry out his plans for the magazine he needed music for its pages — not music already published, but something new that would meet at once the need of the teachers he wanted to help. This need compelled him to secure and publish music, first in his beloved *Etude* and afterwards separately, but with Mr. Presser *the magazine came first*, the rest followed. The periodical was the pivotal center about which in ever widening circles the rest of the business revolved.

Nobody had ever worked in this way before. Musical magazines had come and gone, most of them as house-organs for publishers where the music-publishing came first, and the magazine second, as an adjunct or prop to the business. With Mr. Presser, *The Etude* was the business itself, the music-publishing but the outcome of the magazine. Theodore Presser's unique and significant position in the music-life of America is due to his loyalty to his own vision worked out on individual lines.

He never forgot the struggling small-town music-teacher, his magazine carried her a message, and when she wanted music he made it easy for her to get it. He trusted her, he gave her long credit and low prices. Look at the result of this policy today with a magazine that in circulation far excels the combined distribution of all other music periodicals everywhere, while the Presser yearly output of new publications of music and music-books has been greater in volume than that of any other publisher in the world.

That potential million in pluck and energy naturally and logically expanded into a large fortune, which Mr. Presser decided to dedicate to the assistance of those who had devoted their lives to music and to the advancement of the art. The first manifestation of this was the *Home for Retired Music-Teachers* now at Germantown, where it occupies a property valued at one-half million dollars. This was founded in 1906. In 1916 he decided to consolidate his other private philanthropies and founded *The Presser Foundation*, which now embraces four major departments: I. The Presser Home. II. Department of Relief for Deserving Musicians. III. Department of Music Scholarships at Colleges. Through this department over five thousand students have already been assisted in securing musical educations. The Foundation makes grants only to colleges which in turn have full power to select eligible students. Over two hundred colleges have these scholarships, each amounting to $250. IV. The Department of Music Buildings at Colleges, which has helped many colleges in the erection of suitable music buildings.

In 1886 *The Etude* and the music-publishing business (Theodore Presser) were moved to Chestnut Street above Seventeenth, where at Nos. 1712-1714 they now occupy a considerable portion of that block in the heart of Philadelphia.

In October, 1925, Theodore Presser passed on and James Francis Cooke, editor of *The Etude* and president of the Presser Foundation, became president of the company. In April, 1930, the Presser Company enriched their catalog by the purchase of the John Church Company of Cincinnati, a house established in 1860 by Oliver Ditson. In February, 1931, the great catalog of Oliver Ditson Company of Boston was purchased from the trustees of the estate of the late Charles H. Ditson. The addition of these two important properties, added to their already extensive catalog, makes the Theodore Presser Company the owner of the largest music-publishing combination in the United States.

BALTIMORE PUBLISHERS

Baltimore's pioneer publisher, Joseph Carr, who opened his Musical Repository in 1794, carried on into the nineteenth century, and his successors were active throughout the century.

From 1800 to 1805 Joseph Carr had charge of the music at Old St. Paul's Parish in Baltimore, while his son Thomas was organist of Christ Church from 1798 to 1811 inclusive. To this son, Joseph conveyed the ownership of his music-store and publishing house in September, 1819, dying a month later in his eightieth year. In 1822 Thomas Carr apparently gave up the business or sold it to George Willig, the Philadelphia publisher, who set up a music-store at 71 Baltimore Street in 1823. Thomas Carr then moved to Philadelphia where he is listed as "professor and vender of music" to 1837, and then as "professor of music" to the year of his death, 1849.

In 1829 the Willig firm is listed as George Willig, Jr., at 74 Baltimore Street. Evidently Mr. Willig senior, being fully occupied by his Philadelphia business, put the Baltimore establishment into the hands of his Philadelphia-born son, George, Jr. In 1831 the business moved to 149 Baltimore Street, removing to No. 197 in 1845, and to No. 1 North Charles Street in 1858. In 1868 Mr. Willig's sons Henry and Joseph E. Willig were added to the firm, which then became George Willig & Co. The father died December 10, 1874, and the sons carried on the business until 1910, when it was taken over by the G. Fred Kranz Music Company at 327 North Charles Street.

One of the earliest music-publishers in Baltimore was John Cole, born in Tewksbury, England, in 1774. He came to Baltimore in 1786 as a boy of twelve, and not only composed and taught music but learned the printer's trade and became a book-seller and then a music-publisher. He began to publish music some time prior to 1808. In 1835 he associated his son George T. Cole with him as John Cole & Son at 137 Baltimore Street, and in May, 1839, they were succeeded by Frederick D. Benteen. William C. Miller was taken into partnership in 1853, or earlier, and the firm became Benteen & Co. at 181 Baltimore Street. In 1855, or 1856, Joseph R. Beacham entered the firm, which then became Miller & Beacham. Mr. Beacham disappears from the directory after 1863. In 1872, or soon after, their catalog together with that of Benteen & Co. and whatever was left of the Cole catalog was taken over by Oliver Ditson & Co. of Boston, thus linking this historic house to the first decade of the nineteenth century in Baltimore's story of music-publishing. In 1847 Henry C. McCaffrey, who had been clerk in a music-store, set up in business for himself. In 1853 he was located at 189 Baltimore Street. From 1858 to 1878 he was located at 209 Baltimore Street, moving in 1879 to 7 North Charles Street. Here, and then at No. 9, he continued until 1895, when he turned over his catalog to Oliver Ditson & Co.

NEW YORK PUBLISHERS

The three eighteenth century publishers who carried on in the nineteenth century have been mentioned in an earlier chapter: George Gilfert, the violin player, whose Musical Magazine at 177 Broadway and in 1804 at 13 Maiden Lane, continued until 1814; John Paff who was active at shifting addresses on Broadway,

Maiden Lane, and Park Street until 1817, when his music-store was located at 18 Wall Street; and James Hewitt, violinist, composer, conductor, concert-manager, and publisher, whose shop was at 59 Maiden Lane in 1811. His talents as a musician and fine social standing gave him pre-eminence. His name disappears from the directories 1812-1817, but reappears in 1818 and 1819 merely as "musician." Evidently the senior Hewitt went out of business late in 1811, or early in 1812, but his son, as James L. Hewitt & Co., who in 1825-1829 was a Boston publisher, opened a music-store in 1830 and published music at 137 Broadway. James Hewitt the elder died in Boston in 1827. In 1839-1841 as Hewitt & Jaques they were at 239 Broadway, but from 1842 until 1847 as James L. Hewitt & Co., and in 1844 as James L. Hewitt, they were at various Broadway addresses. The name disappears from the directory after 1847.

These early publishers reprinted the most popular songs and piano pieces from London, mostly songs; and now and then the work of a local musician. The engraving was crude and the music hand-printed without title-page or date. Although national copyright was enacted in 1790, and in 1802 the notice of copyright was required, the custom of printing the date did not follow until well into the nineteenth century. In his research the writer came across a song by Gilfert, *For then I had not learned to love*, published by E. Riley, New York, bearing the notice: "Copyrighted June 15, in the thirty-eighth year of the independence of the United States of America," in other words 1814.

A few titles will indicate the type of music in vogue in this sentimental period: *Arabella the Caledonian Maid*, *The Contented Cottager* (composers not mentioned, as was often the case) and Shields' song, *Lovely Jane*, issued by Gilfert; Pucitta's *Strike the Cymbal* and Cope's song, *Mark the busy insect playing*, issued by Paff; Arne's *The Soldier tired*, Davy's *Crazy Jane* (both favorites), Kelly's *Ah! what is the bosom's commotion*, and Hewitt's own thrilling song, *Five chiefs of renown by his hatchet lay dead*, published by Hewitt.

One of the earliest organ-builders in New York was John Geib, who is listed as such in 1798, and as John Geib & Co. in 1800. He was son of the London piano-maker of the same name. Adam, his brother, a music-teacher, and his own son William became associated with him later, for in 1816 John and Adam Geib & Co. had a music-store and sold pianos at 23 Maiden Lane where they also published music. This firm with some changes continued at this address until 1843, and with various moves existed until 1872; though from 1842 their chief if not sole business was as piano-makers and dealers. The fact that a portion of the publishing catalog of Geib & Walker (1829-1843) was absorbed by the house of S. T. Gordon links this early firm to the present day.

Mention must be made of Edward Riley, the music-teacher and engraver, who first appears in the directory of 1806. Whether he was the Edward Riley who from 1799 to 1802 published and engraved music in London is probable though not definitely known; but his name appears as engraver on much music of the period, and Riley & Adams were copper-plate printers at 23 and also 29 Chatham Street, while E. Riley from 1814 to 1831 was a music-publisher at the same address. In 1832 his widow Elizabeth carried on the music-store at 29 Chatham Street, followed by the sons Edward C. and Frederick, who continued the business until 1851 when they were succeeded by J. E. Gould & Co., then by Gould & Berry, who in 1854 were absorbed by Berry & Gordon (Thomas S. Berry and Stephen T. Gordon) at 297 Broadway. (Mr. Gordon's further career is given on page 102.)

Another pioneer publisher was the French clarinettist, singer, and composer, William Dubois, who came to this country about 1795. He opened a music-store at 33 White Street according to the directory of 1813, and on Broadway as Dubois & Stodart (1822-1834), Dubois & Bacon (1835-1838), then alone (1839-1849), Dubois & Warriner (1850-1852), and again by himself until 1854.

A pioneer house linked to present-day activities is that of John Firth, born in England in 1789, who came to New York and from 1815 to 1820 made and dealt in musical instruments. In the latter year with William Hall as partner they published music under the name of Firth & Hall at 362 Pearl Street. In

1832 Sylvanus B. Pond, who in 1820 had formed in Albany, N. Y., the firm of Meacham & Pond, moved to New York at the invitation of Firth & Hall, and in the latter part of the year the firm of Firth, Hall & Pond was established at No. 1 Franklin Square in a house formerly occupied by General Washington. In 1848 General Hall withdrew to form the firm of William Hall & Son at 239 Broadway, which moved in 1859 to No. 543 and in 1871 to No. 751 Broadway, until in 1875 their catalog was purchased by Oliver Ditson & Co. of Boston.

Meanwhile Firth, Pond & Co. continued at No. 1 Franklin Square, and in 1850 S. B. Pond retired, turning over his interests to his son William A. Pond. In 1856 the firm moved to 547 Broadway. In January, 1863, John Firth withdrew and as Firth, Son & Co. published music at 563 Broadway until 1866 when as Thaddeus Firth the business ceased. Part of the catalog of Firth, Pond & Co. was taken over by S. T. Gordon, but the music-plates and stock of Firth, Son & Co. were purchased on March 4, 1867, by Oliver Ditson & Co. of Boston. This led Mr. Ditson to send his eldest son Charles to New York to open at 563 Broadway a branch house under the name of Chas. H. Ditson & Co. The old Firth quarters proving inadequate they moved in a few months to 711 Broadway, and in 1878 to 843 Broadway, for the purchase of the business of William Hall & Son in 1875 and that of J. L. Peters in 1877 again necessitated larger quarters. From 1883 Chas. H. Ditson & Co. were at 867 Broadway until Mr. C. H. Ditson erected the new Ditson building at 8-10-12 East Thirty-fourth Street, into which the firm moved in 1907, where it remained until February, 1931, when, after the death of Mr. Ditson, the Oliver Ditson Company was purchased by the Theodore Presser Company.

On January 31, 1863, after dissolving the firm of Firth, Pond & Co., William A. Pond with John Mayell as partner formed the firm of William A. Pond & Co., which continued at the old location, 547 Broadway, until 1877 when they moved to 25 Union Square where the business grew and prospered. It was in 1843 that organized negro minstrelsy came into existence and grew rapidly into popularity. Edwin T. Christy with his famous troupe was the man who more than any other stereotyped the minstrel show. His minstrels and many similar companies carried the songs they made popular all over the land, and Pond & Co. were among the first to publish them.

When Stephen Foster began to write his unique songs Colonel Pond made a five-year contract with him that proved so satisfactory to both that it was renewed three times in succession. Foster's much loved song, *Old Folks at Home*, sold in one month over 100,000 copies, something never before heard of. The house of William A. Pond & Co. moved in 1896 to 124 Fifth Avenue, in 1898 to 148 Fifth Avenue, and in 1909 to 18 West Thirty-seventh Street, where the business is at present conducted by Mr. G. Warren Pond, son of William A. Pond.

Of John Appel (1812-1815); Joseph F. Atwill (1833-1850); Thomas Birch, music-engraver and printer as well as publisher (1820-1842); Charles E. Horn, known today as the composer of the charming song, *I'd be a butterfly*, (1839-1843); Edward I. Jaques and his brothers James M. and John D. (1839-1857); William E. Millet and his sons (1835-1879); Horace Waters, Joseph Willson (1815-1821), and William C. Peters, mention should be made.

The publishers of the period 1820-1840 reprinted the songs of the composers then popular — Bishop, Horn, Cooke, Alexander Lee, John Barnett, Samuel Lover, and Henry Russell, whose descriptive ballads, *The Maniac*, *The Ship on Fire*, and *The Gambler's Wife* were being sung with melodramatic fervor in fashionable drawing-rooms.

It was in 1819 that Rossini's *Barber of Seville* was sung in English in New York; in 1823 Mozart's *Marriage of Figaro* was also given in English, and Weber's *Der Freischütz* in 1825. It was in this same year that Garcia's opera company, including the great Malibran, introduced Italian opera to New York in a series of seventy-nine performances.

From this date on began the zest for operatic airs, transcriptions, and fantasias which gradually replaced the simpler "airs with variations" of the preceding period, and the simpler songs from English ballad-operas. The years from 1820 to 1840 also saw considerable development in the manufacture of pianos and organs, an evidence of the constant growth in musical activity.

A sturdy New Hampshire boy of musical bent, Stephen T. Gordon, went before his father's death to Boston at the time when Lowell Mason was its dominant figure. Through Mason's aid and friendly advice he went to Hartford, Conn., where he was further encouraged by Dudley Buck. In 1846 young Gordon started publishing music in New York. In 1854 with the financial co-operation of Oliver Ditson and the partnership of J. E. Gould and T. S. Berry, whose business as Gould & Berry was merged with his, S. T. Gordon & Co. moved to the corner of Broadway and Spring Street. In May, 1855, Gordon bought out his partners, at the same time purchasing the catalog of Russel & Tolman of Boston. By 1861 S. T. Gordon, then at 706 Broadway, had absorbed the catalogs of twenty-four publishers. In 1876 Mr. Gordon took his son Hamilton S. into partnership under the name of S. T. Gordon & Son. After the death of the senior Gordon in December, 1890, the business was continued by Hamilton S. Gordon, and since his death in June, 1914, the business has been carried on at 141-145 West Thirty-sixth Street, by the three grandsons of its founder—Leslie, Hamilton A., and Herbert Gordon. Among the widely known publications of the house are the songs, *Silver threads among the gold*, by H. P.

Danks, *Under the daisies*, by Harrison Millard, and some of the latter's popular masses.

In 1844 Scharfenberg & Luis opened a music-store at 361 Broadway, specializing in foreign music and doing some publishing. They continued in business until 1866, by which time they had in the upward trend reached No. 758 Broadway. They are mentioned because they took into their employ a young man who was destined to become a great national figure in music publishing — Gustav Schirmer. Born in Königsee, Saxony, September 19, 1829, the son of a piano-maker, he came to New York a boy of eight in 1837. In 1854 he became manager for Kerksieg & Breusing, a house established in 1848 at 421 Broadway. At about this same date Mr. Evich Kerksieg seems to have withdrawn, for the business was carried on alone by Charles Breusing until 1861 when it was bought out by Gustav Schirmer and B. Beer, who for five years carried on the business as Beer & Schirmer at 701 Broadway.

In 1866 Mr. Schirmer obtained complete control and as G. Schirmer continued the business at the same address until his constant expansion compelled him to erect in 1880 the building at 35 Union Square. Here the ever increasing business continued for nearly thirty

Gustav Schirmer

years. Finally, having again outgrown its quarters and following the general uptown trend of New York's retail trade, the firm erected in 1909 the seven-story fireproof building at No. 3 East Forty-third Street it occupies today.

In was in 1885 that Mr. Schirmer's two sons Gustave, Jr. (1864-1907) and Rudolph E. (1859-1919) became partners in the business, making it one of the great music-houses of the world.

The founder of the house dying on August 6, 1893, the business was incorporated as G. Schirmer, Inc., with the senior son Rudolph as president, a position he maintained until his death, August 20, 1919. His nephew Gustave Schirmer, 3d, succeeded him until, upon his resignation, April 27, 1921, Mr. W. Rodman Fay was elected president, and Mr. Oscar G. Sonneck, musicologist, critic, and editor was made vice-president, a position he held until his death, October 30, 1928. Mr. Carl Engel became president on May 7, 1929; an office he relinquished in 1932 in order to resume his important duties as chief of the music division of the Library of Congress in Washington, D. C. His successor Mr. Hermann Irion took office January 1, 1933.

The name of the Saxon boy who arrived in New York on the ship, *Antonene*, October 8, 1837, has now for many years been stamped on music of quality, for it was his aim and the aim of those who followed him to keep pace with the ever increasing demand for the best in music, issued in a style befitting its worth.

Mention should be made of the establishment in 1915 of *The Musical Quarterly* under the editorship of Mr. O. G. Sonneck. This unique and idealistic magazine of high quality and international scope treats musical topics in scholarly fashion from an historical and critical basis. Upon the death of Mr. Sonneck, October 30, 1928, the editorship was put into the able hands of Dr. Carl Engel, composer, musicologist, and littérateur.

In 1892 two energetic and experienced music-clerks George Belder and George C. Luckhardt joined their forces and, as Luckhardt & Belder, opened a music-shop at 10 East Sixteenth Street and began to publish music. In 1913 Mr. Belder passed on, and on May 23, 1925, the catalog was purchased by the young publishing firm of Harold Flammer, Inc., which had been established on June 6, 1917. Mr. Flammer's fast-growing catalog was taken over as a distinct unit by G. Schirmer, Inc. on November 1, 1929, and on the same day Mr. Flammer became vice-president and business manager of G. Schirmer, Inc.

In 1872 Carl Fischer, a vigorous young Saxon of twenty-three, trained in the manufacture and sale of musical instruments, came to New York and immediately engaged in the music-business at 79 East Fourth Street. As he was a performer on the violin, double-bass, French horn, and bassoon he at first supplemented the earnings of his then modest business by professional engagements. His sale of band and orchestral instruments led him at once to publish music for them and, from the beginning, these two departments have grown together to their present great proportions. His first publication was an arrangement of a Strauss waltz for orchestra, for he had discovered the great lack of properly arranged orchestra music especially for small instrumental combinations. Among the very first issues for military

Carl Fischer

band was the *Turkish Patrol*, by Michaelis, and an arrangement of the *Poet and Peasant* overture by Suppé. In 1878 the business was moved to 386 Bowery, in 1880 to 26 Fourth Avenue, and in 1882 the need of still larger quarters caused the removal to Cooper Square.

The strength of the catalog in band and orchestra music led Carl Fischer to establish in 1885, *The Metronome*, a journal devoted to the interests of this expanding field. From band and orchestra music Carl Fischer gradually widened the scope of his publications to cover every department of musical activity. This led to the establishment, January, 1907, of *The Musical Observer*, a monthly magazine for teachers, students, and lovers of music. In 1922 the fiftieth anniversary of the founding of the house was celebrated and on February 14,

1923, its founder, born December 7, 1849, passed on. His son Walter S. Fischer, long associated with his father in the management of the business, succeeded him as head of the house. The cramped quarters of the building on Cooper Square, occupied with additions since 1882, led to the erection of a large twelve-story building next door, into which the house moved in September, 1923. In October, 1930, the firm took over the American representation of the music publications of the Oxford University Press.

It was in 1864 that a young schoolmaster and musician, Joseph Fischer, established in Dayton, Ohio, the firm of J. Fischer & Bro. His experience as an organist, together with his devoutness, interested him naturally in music for the Catholic church, and it was the offer of the position as organist at the church of the Most Holy Redeemer in 1876 which brought him and his then modest publishing-business to New York. His ardor for church music led him to specialize in this branch, particularly in music for the Catholic services. In 1876 the firm was located at 226 East Fourth Street. In 1884 J. Fischer & Bro. moved to the Bible House, Astor Place. On the death of Mr. Joseph Fischer in 1901 the business was continued by his two sons, George and Carl T., and in 1906 the present corporation was formed with George Fischer as president and Carl T. Fischer as secretary-treasurer. In 1925, following the uptown trend, they moved to 119 West Fortieth Street. Under their management the house has broadened its field, building up an extensive organ catalog, adding an important list of operettas, and progressing more and more into general publishing.

The firm of Schroeder & Gunther, Inc. was founded in 1891 in New York City by John Henry Schroeder. He began business at 12 East Sixteenth Street as a combination publishing and retail music company under the firm name of J. H. Schroeder. Associated with the business was Mr. John Ferdinand Schroeder, a brother, who fell heir to the business in 1916 on the death of Mr. John Henry Schroeder. The original firm name was continued until 1920 when Emil A. Gunther purchased a half-interest in the business, whereupon the firm became a partnership under the name of Schroeder & Gunther. In 1921 a son Edwin L. Gunther joined the firm. In 1924 the partnership incorporated under the name of Schroeder & Gunther, Inc., with three stockholders, namely, John F. Schroeder, Emil A. Gunther, and his son Edwin L. Gunther.

From the beginning this firm has pursued a policy of publishing educational material and in later years specialized almost exclusively in the publication of piano-teaching material. Since 1901 the firm has been located at 6 East Forty-fifth Street.

Born in Brighton, England, in 1868 Mr. H. Willard Gray came to New York in 1894 as the American agent for the historic London publishers, Novello, Ewer & Co., founded in 1811. Mr. Gray's headquarters were first at 21 East Seventeenth Street. In 1906 the H. W.

Gray Company was formed and purchased the American branch of Novello, Ewer & Co. Mr. Gray was elected president of the company, which office he still holds. In 1913 the company moved to 2 West Forty-fifth Street, and in 1923 to 159 East Forty-eighth Street, the present offices. In 1901 the firm began the publication of the *Church Music Review*, as the official organ of the American Guild of Organists. The name was changed to the *New Music Review and Church Music Review* in 1904. In 1922 the Gray Company took over the publication of the *American Organ Quarterly*. From its inception the house has made, as its specialty, music for the church and has published much choir music by American composers.

Another prominent London publisher, Boosey & Co., Ltd., established their own agency in 1892 at 9 East Seventeenth Street, moving in June, 1925, to Steinway Hall, 113 West Fifty-seventh Street. They have enriched their catalog by publishing quite a number of songs and duets by American composers.

The great Italian music-publishers, G. Ricordi & Co., established in Milan in 1808, opened a branch in New York at 9 East Seventeenth Street in 1897. Two years later, under the management of George Maxwell, they began to publish American compositions and have continued to do so ever since. Mr. George Maxwell died in Paris on June 29, 1931, and was succeeded as managing director by Dr. Renato Tasselli, who came to New York from the London branch of

Ricordi & Co. In order that it might more freely develop its growing catalog of the works of American composers, the New York branch was converted into a corporation in 1911 and the headquarters were moved to 14 East Forty-third Street. In 1932 the establishment removed to 12 West Forty-fifth Street, where it is now located.

∴

Reference has already been made to the rise of negro minstrelsy in the eighteen-forties. The songs carried over the land by this popular form of entertainment sung by the Christy Minstrels in the early period, and by Harrigan and Hart, and Thatcher, Primrose and West in the closing period, to mention but three of a host of such groups, form part of the history of music-publishing in this country, but when gorgeousness and glitter took the place of negro characterization the minstrel show declined and died. It had degenerated into a musical variety entertainment which in its artificiality lost touch with plantation life.

Its native place was taken by a form of entertainment imported from the cafés of Paris and the music-halls of London — the vaudeville — which brought in its train a new type of song and with it the so-called "popular" publisher came into being.

When Julius P. Witmark, then the most popular boy soprano in vaudeville, was filling an eight months' engagement at the Eden Musée on Twenty-third Street, New York, at that time the largest house of its kind in the country, he "made" the song, *Always take a mother's advice*. It was published by the Willis Woodward Company, then the biggest factor in minstrel and popular songs. Young Witmark was so dissatisfied with the treatment he received from this concern that he determined to start music-publishing with his musical brothers.

So when Julius was twelve and Isidore almost fifteen they set up the type and printed their first music at home. The two boys, assisted by their younger brothers, then sold or tried to sell their music to the stores. The firm name was Witmark Brothers but because as minors they could get no bank account under this name they changed it to M. Witmark & Sons.

The first song they issued was written by Isidore Witmark, *I'll answer that question tomorrow*, published in 1885. A later success, also written by Isidore, was *A mother is a mother after all*. Julius had made most of his success singing "mother" songs, and as a boy baritone in 1886 he continued on this line. Later Julius Witmark made a hit with *The picture that's turned to the wall*, which he sang for two years in Hoyt's show, *A trip to Chinatown*. To successful publishing of "popular" music the Witmarks added a type of song midway between the "art-song" and the "popular" song. Known as the "semi-popular" song it is characterized by words of the sentimental or ballad type with music that is simple, singable, and melodious.

Located for many years at 144-146 West Thirty-seventh Street, in July, 1913, the house of M. Witmark & Sons moved into their new building at 1650 Broadway. On January 1, 1919, the business was purchased by Warner Brothers, but it continues to operate under the original firm name at 1650 Broadway with an educational department at 619 West Fifty-fourth Street. Mr. Julius Witmark died June 14, 1929.

Obviously music-publishers are naturally divided by diverse aims and methods into two distinct types: the so-called "standard publisher" and the "popular publisher." The first group is primarily educational in aim, in that it publishes music and books of pedagogic value, and also music that has no avowed educational purpose, for its *raison d'être* is primarily aesthetic, although its sale depends more upon the music-teacher than upon that somewhat nondescript person, "the music-lover." The second group is not at all concerned with music-pedagogy or so-called "art-music," but with music written for no other purpose than entertainment.

The first publishes staple, comparatively slow-going music, the sale of which may cover a long period of years. The second type issues, or seeks to issue, "hits" which are vigorously exploited by every possible means, have an immediate and ephemeral success sometimes running into sales of a million or more, then disappear. This is of course a speculative game with large and quick returns, and also large losses. In the nature of things publishing of this type is linked directly to the stage and, as New York is the stage and vaudeville booking and production center of the country, the "Broadway" publisher finds his natural habitat there. Perhaps it was a Chicago critic who first dubbed these publishers "Denizens of Tin-Pan-Alley"; at any rate the name has stuck and the press representative of one of the most successful of them does not hesitate to use it in describing his own firm.

In September, 1897, a young star corset salesman, Leo Feist by name, with a knack for writing catchy airs, having had his efforts at writing a popular song turned down, hired a small room at 1227 Broadway and with a piano and a partner began publishing his own song, *Does true love ever run smooth?*

That one-room office grew into two buildings with branches in all the principal cities. In recent years the publisher of *Smoky Mokes, Anona, Peg o' my heart, Goodbye Broadway, Over there, Three o'clock in the morning, Ramona, My blue Heaven,* and many other successes, has also become a factor in the publication of musical comedies such as *Irene, Blossom Time,* and *Rio Rita.* Though not generally known, Mr. Feist is the owner of the low-priced *Century Edition* of standard and "classical" music. The present location of Leo Feist, Inc., is at 56 Cooper Square.

Lack of space forbids more than mention here of Irving Berlin, Inc.; T. B. Harms, Inc.; Shapiro, Bernstein & Co., Inc.; Remick Music Corp.; Robbins Music Corp., and E. B. Marks Music Company.

The story of "Popular Music" in America has its

indisputable place in any complete history of American music, for the songs of forty-year old Tin-Pan-Alley record, with a humor that never suffers from over-refinement, or a pathos that is often bathos, the passing moods and modes and noisy trivialities of the seething human mass that nightly surges up the Great White Way. The Alley's strident songs and nervous dance-tunes, its blurbs and ballads and banalities are as evanescent as the encircling smoke in which they are ground out in accordance with constantly changing recipes and anti-routine formulas. In one essential, however, there is no change, for this frankly commercial pursuit involves a ceaseless and eager following of the taste of the crowd — the indiscriminate and undiscriminating crowd — an inseparable part of the American scene.

An illuminating essay on the unconscious growth of public taste in its gradual acceptance of harmonic subtlety and rhythmic variety might be based on an analysis of the great popular successes from the plain, even-gaited rhythms and simple harmonies of the songs of the eighteen-sixties to the complicated rhythms, augmented triads, chords of the ninth and secondary sevenths of the present-day vogue.

BOSTON PUBLISHERS

Of the two pioneer publishers, Peter Albrecht von Hagen and Gottlieb Graupner, account has been given in an earlier chapter.

Another pioneer, Francis Mallet, singer, organist, and pianist in Boston from 1793 to 1832 was for a time associated with Graupner in his "Conservatorio" and in publishing as Graupner & Mallet. After withdrawing from this connection, Mallet in 1805-1807 had his own music-shop in Devonshire Street, where he did some publishing. Judging from what has survived, Graupner's output was more extended than that of his predecessor and contemporary von Hagen, and he ventured to publish some larger and more important works.

The followers of these doughty pioneers were more cautious. To combine the selling of music with books was natural, but the curious combination of music and umbrellas seems peculiar to Boston in the period 1825-1845. John Ashton, Jr., and John Ashton & Co. (E. H. Wade) umbrella-makers, from 1820-1843 at 18 Marlboro Street and 197 Washington Street, may have set the fashion of adding music and musical instruments to their stock in trade, a step they took in 1825. They were followed by Frederick Lane, the umbrella-man of Court Street, 1821-1837; Henry Prentiss who, having been an umbrella-maker from 1825 to 1833 on Court Street, added pianos and music in 1834 and published music as well until 1845; and Charles H. Keith, another Court Street umbrella-maker from 1833, who added music and instruments to his stock in 1835, in 1840 took in a partner for two years as Keith & Moore, and as music-dealer and publisher under his own name continued until 1846, when the catalog was purchased by Oliver Ditson & Co. A shorter-lived umbrella and music-store was that of a former partner of John Ashton, Eben H. Wade, who, at 197 Washington Street, did some publishing between 1847 and 1851.

A short-lived but important concern, James L. Hewitt & Co. (James A. Dickson) 1825-1829, at No. 34 Market Street, advertised in September, 1826, "Elegant London Piano Fortes, etc.," and in another column on the same page:

"DAY AND MARTIN, REAL JAPAN BLACKING, 100 casks of the above, variously assorted always kept on hand, for sale by Wholesale or Retail at the Music Saloon No. 34 & 36 Market St., Boston."

Mr. Dickson, prior to joining this firm, had a "Music Saloon" from 1816 and when James L. Hewitt moved to New York, Dickson continued alone, moving in 1830 to No. 34 Cornhill. His name disappears after 1839.

Following the umbrella period are two publishers who must be mentioned because they were at times in friendly association and because both are linked directly to the present. One was Charles Bradlee who began music-publishing in 1829 at 164 Washington Street and continued at various addresses until 1846, after which his name disappears from the Boston directory. His catalog was taken over by Oliver Ditson. The other publisher was Samuel H. Parker who in April, 1811, took over the Union Circulating Library and shop of William Blagrove at No. 3 School Street. This business was the direct successor of Ebenezer Battelle's Boston Book Store, opened in 1783 at No. 8 State Street. Parker's relationship with Oliver Ditson, who became his successor, has already been told. His interest in the firm of Parker & Ditson was purchased by the junior partner in 1842.

Of the mid-century period only Oliver Ditson & Co. survived. Mention must be made of W. H. Oakes at 383½ Washington Street (1840-1851), and A. & J. P. Ordway at 339 Washington Street (1846-1849) whose catalog was purchased by Oliver Ditson. More important and longer-lived was George P. Reed and his various successors. In 1839 Mr. Reed opened his music-store at 17 Tremont Street where he published music. In 1850 he took his chief clerk, George D. Russell, into partnership as George P. Reed & Co. In 1859 Mr. Russell left Mr. Reed to go into partnership with Nathan Richardson, who had owned a "Musical Exchange" since 1854, as Russell & Richardson at 291 Washington Street, successors to G. P. Reed & Co. and Nathan Richardson. For a short time the firm was known as Russell & Fuller. In 1859 Richardson withdrew and Henry Tolman, dealer in musical instruments and umbrellas, became partner as Russell & Tolman. They were succeeded by Henry Tolman & Co. at 291 Washington Street.

In 1863 Joseph M. Russell, who since 1850 had

conducted a rival establishment at 61 Court Street with P. S. Gilmore, the noted bandmaster, as partner, and then as Russell & Patee at 108 Tremont Street, joined his brother George and the firm became G. D. Russell & Co. at 126 Tremont Street. In 1877 they separated, Joseph M. going to 59 Bromfield Street. In 1884 they reunited as Russell Bros. at 126 Tremont Street, but in two or three years they again separated, Joseph M. going to 10 Hamilton Place. After 1889 his name disappears. Meanwhile G. D. Russell continued at 126 Tremont Street until 1888 when, upon the death of Mr. Russell, the extensive catalog and business was taken over by Oliver Ditson & Co. The catalog contained much of musical worth. This firm of varied fortune is mentioned not only for their forty-nine years of activity, but because in their best days in the early seventies they employed, in their retail department, a young man destined to make a distinguished place for himself among American publishers. This young man, Arthur Paul Schmidt, born in Altoona, Germany, April 1, 1846, came to Boston in January, 1866. In 1876 he opened a retail music-store at No. 40 Winter Street and, though at first he specialized in the importation of foreign music, he saw with discerning eye the dawning era of the native composer and more and more identified himself with it. Mr. Schmidt's first publication was issued in 1877, and from that time until his death, May 5, 1921, he increasingly devoted his time and energy to the development of American music.

With remarkable vision he was the first to recognize the gifts of Paine, Chadwick, Foote, MacDowell, Mrs. Beach, and others. Familiar as these names are to us now, Mr. Schmidt was willing to publish their works before they had achieved their present notable place in American music, and when such publications were a decided risk, a venture made on faith in the future of this uncommercial group. The publication in 1880 of John K. Paine's *Spring Symphony* marked the first issue in this country of the score and parts of a large orchestral work by a native composer. Arthur Foote's *Francesca da Rimini*, G. W. Chadwick's second and third Symphonies, not to mention other orchestral works and chamber-music, were products of those early days. In order to devote the whole of his time to the publishing business Mr. Schmidt in 1889 sold out his retail business, then at 13 and 15 West Street, to Miles & Thompson, succeeded later by C. W. Thompson & Co. It was then he moved to 154 Tremont Street, later to 146 Boylston Street, and in April, 1903, to No. 120 where the firm now is. It was in 1888 that Edward MacDowell returned from twelve years' absence in Europe, and was so little known in his own country he could find no New York house willing to risk the publication of his works.

Arthur Paul Schmidt

Here again Mr. Schmidt ventured where others hesitated, and brought out the long series of compositions that have since given MacDowell his pre-eminent place in American music.

While other publishers were continually reprinting the non-copyright and therefore competitive works of foreign composers, Mr. Schmidt's consistent policy was devoted to building up a notable catalog of copyright music. While foreign writers of merit are included, the great bulk of the Schmidt catalog is the work of native composers.

In 1916 Mr. Schmidt in great measure withdrew from active participation in the business, and formed the Arthur P. Schmidt Company of his co-workers and tried helpers—Mr. Harry B. Crosby, Mr. Henry R. Austin, and Miss Florence J. Emery. On May 5, 1921, with his house in order and his work as champion of the American composer done, Arthur P. Schmidt passed on.

The firm of Koppitz, Prüffer & Co. began business at 30 West Street in 1869. Carl Prüffer had for three years been foreign music-clerk for Oliver Ditson & Co., and Charles Koppitz was musical director of Selwyn's Theatre and later of the Globe Theatre. The firm continued as Carl Prüffer until soon after his death, December 16, 1886, it was absorbed by Oliver Ditson & Co.

Charles A. White, born in Dighton, Mass., played the violin at an early age and starting out as a dancing-master, was at one time professor of dancing and fencing at the United States Naval Academy when it was located at Newport, R. I. It was at this time that he wrote a number of successful songs which were published by Oliver Ditson & Co. The popularity of his songs led him in 1868 to form with W. Frank Smith, previously a retail clerk of Ditson's, and John F. Perry of New Bedford, the publishing firm of White, Smith & Perry at 298 and 300 Washington Street. In 1874 Mr. Perry withdrew and the firm continued as White, Smith & Co., while John F. Perry carried on as a separate dealer in music and pianos until 1883.

It was in this period that Mr. C. A. White's songs, *Put me in my little bed*, *I'm goin' back to Dixie*, *When the leaves begin to turn* and, best known of all, *Marguerite*, reached a nation-wide sale. During his career Mr. White wrote, it is reported, more than fifteen hundred compositions, many of them published under various pen-names.

Upon the death of Mr. Smith in June, 1891, his interests were bought by Mr. White who then took his son Daniel L. White into partnership. On the death of Mr. C. A. White in January, 1892, the corporation styled the White-Smith Music Company was formed with Daniel L. White as president. Upon his death in August, 1918, his only son Charles A. White, grandson of the founder, became and still is president of the company. Their office and music-printing establishment were for many years located at 62 and 64 Stanhope Street, but in September, 1921, they moved to 40-44 Winchester Street, where they are still located.

Gustave Schirmer, Jr., the second son of the founder of the great publishing house of G. Schirmer, was born in New York, February 18, 1864. At the age of seventeen he was sent abroad for a thorough apprenticeship in music-publishing and for the study of music itself. After five years' preparation he returned to this country and in the autumn of 1885 established the Boston Music Company at No. 2 Beacon Street, where the young man of twenty-one was everything from president to bookkeeper and office-boy. In 1886 G. Schirmer, Jr., issued his first publication, a *Concert Etude*, by Arthur Whiting. In the latter part of this year he moved to 28 West Street, and four or five years later expanding business made the occupation of No. 26 West Street necessary.

Gustave Schirmer, Jr.

In 1888 Mr. Schirmer's important association with Ethelbert Nevin began with the publication of his three songs, Opus 3 — *Deep in a rose's glowing heart*, *One Spring morning*, and *Doris*. Nevin's widely popular *Sketch Book* was issued this year, followed in 1891 with *Water Scenes*, containing the enormously popular *Narcissus*. When Nevin wrote the *Rosary* he happened to be in New York and so submitted it to Mr. Rudolph

Schirmer. The latter saw his brother Gustave the next day and handing the manuscript to him said: "Here's a charming little song which I think you should be permitted to publish in the Boston Music Company catalog, for you have most of Mr. Nevin's other compositions." With these words he turned to G. Schirmer, Jr., the song which has sold the greatest number of copies recorded in modern times. Thus upon a generous impulse one brother gave a fortune to the other.

In 1890, owing to the serious illness of Gustav Schirmer, Senior, the son returned to New York to carry on with his brother Rudolph the management of G. Schirmer, Inc.

The sudden taking off of Gustave Schirmer, Jr., July 15, 1907, robbed American publishers of a man of high ideals and catholic taste who looked upon music-publishing not as a mere business for profit but as a profession and a service to the art he himself loved so deeply and genuinely.

Upon his death the control of the Boston Music Company passed into the hands of his son Gustave who, on December 1, 1922, moved the publication headquarters to 10 East Forty-fourth Street, New York, while the business itself was continued at 26 West Street, Boston, until, on March 1, 1926, it was moved to 116 Boylston Street.

The ship that in October, 1837, brought Gustav Schirmer as a boy of eight from Thuringia, Saxony, to New York to found later the publishing house that bears his honored name, brought his younger brother Edward Schirmer, a boy of six. In 1878 Edward's son Ernest C. Schirmer, then thirteen years old, became an apprentice in the music-store of his uncle Gustav at 701 Broadway, New York. In October, 1891, he became business manager of the Boston Music Company founded by his cousin, G. Schirmer, Jr., and was admitted to partnership in January, 1902. In 1917 Mr. Ernest Schirmer withdrew from the Boston Music Company, and in 1921 founded the E. C. Schirmer Music Company at 221 Columbus Avenue, where the business is still located. With the friendly co-operation of Dr. Archibald T. Davison of Harvard University and Mr. Thomas Whitney Surette of Concord, Mass., the company has specialized in publishing choral music of a high type, giving special attention to *a cappella* music.

The reader must have already noted the fact that all of the more important publishing houses have had their origin in the musical knowledge and enthusiasm of their founders. Business routine and ability, both essential to success, develop with experience, but the great publishers were primarily great music-lovers.

The founder of the B. F. Wood Music Company was no exception to this rule. Born in Lewiston, Me., March 27, 1849, where he first studied, he then became a student at the New England Conservatory of Music. Completing his course there he returned to Lewiston, where for some years he taught piano and organ and served as organist and choir-director in the churches of that city and Auburn, Me.

The restrictions that seemed to hamper Mr. Wood's career in those days, and the scarcity of teaching material of the type he needed for his pupils, brought him into contact with Arthur P. Schmidt of Boston and for about three years he was associated with him as his general manager. This experience in publishing, coupled with his own knowledge as a practical teacher, led Mr. Wood to establish, in 1893, the B. F. Wood Music Company, at 110 Boylston Street. In this venture his partner was Mr. John Aiken Preston, also an experienced piano-teacher. The aim of the new house was to supply piano-teachers in particular with an abundance of easy teaching material that combined melodic interest with pedagogic value. On this Mr. Wood concentrated his efforts, supplementing his copyrights with volume reprints of the standard and classic teaching material in the *Edition Wood*, which now numbers over one thousand volumes. Another feature of Mr. Wood's policy was his belief that teachers' needs could best be served by their local dealer. Accordingly he based his selling policy on the protection of the dealer's interests, referring all orders to him.

B. F. Wood

On July 22, 1914, Mr. Preston died, and on July 29, 1922, Mr. B. F. Wood also passed on. The business is now conducted by his nephew Mr. Harold W. Robinson as president, and Mr. W. Deane Preston, Jr., nephew of Mr. Wood's first partner as vice-president. When the business had outgrown its first quarters it was moved to 231 Columbus Avenue, and in 1901 to 246 Summer Street. Still expanding, the firm moved in October, 1920, to its own commodious building at No. 88 St. Stephen Street, where it is still located.

For many years the publication of music for the Catholic church was carried on by the chief publishers in connection with the music they issued for Protestant choirs, but in 1904 the promulgation of the *Motu Proprio* of Pope Pius X inaugurated a reformation in Catholic music, and banned many of the masses of the florid type long popular. This break with conventional usage made the publishing of liturgical music for the Catholic service a specialty. In this significant year, 1904, Mr. James M. McLaughlin, who had been supervisor of music in the Boston schools, and Dr. James A. Reilly, singer and choir-master, formed the firm of McLaughlin & Reilly for the publication of music for the Catholic service. Beginning at 171 Tremont Street, they incorporated in May, 1909, as McLaughlin & Reilly Co., and moved to 100 Boylston Street where they are still located. In 1927 the firm acquired the catalog of William E. Ashmall of Arlington, N. J., founded in 1877, and with it *The Organist's*

Journal. In 1930 they acquired the liturgical catalog of John B. Singenberger of St. Francis, Wis., founded in 1874, and with it *The Caecilia*, a magazine of Catholic church music which they still publish. The Liturgical Music Company, and Catholic Music Publishing Company have also been acquired.

For years Boston has been a center for the publishing of school-music. This is only natural, for it was through the great pioneer Lowell Mason that in 1838 music became a regular branch of study in the public schools of Boston. The rapid extension of music-study in our schools has been met by specialists in this department, such as Ginn & Co.; Silver, Burdett & Co., and C. C. Birchard & Co., all important publishers in this big field.

It was in 1900 that Mr. Clarence C. Birchard, after some years of experience that had made him thoroughly familiar with the school-music situation in our public schools, founded the publishing firm of C. C. Birchard & Co. at 221 Columbus Avenue. Mr. Birchard was convinced that the time had come for the introduction of a better and more serious type of music than had hitherto been supplied American schools. He therefore enlisted the co-operation of some twenty-five of the best American composers who were invited to make choral settings of texts of literary value. The resulting volume, *The Laurel Song Book*, was issued in 1901. The book also included a much larger proportion of art-songs than had hitherto been available in collections of school-music and set a new standard in education. The policy then initiated of issuing for school use music of genuine worth has ever since been maintained and has given the Birchard Company an individual place in its special field. In 1903 the first number was issued in their extensive octavo series for choral singing. In 1913 the Birchard Company entered the field of low-priced assembly song-books in which they have been notably successful. In 1923 they began the publication of music for school orchestras, and followed this step in 1924 by the publication of symphonic works by American composers. Still under the direction of its founder, the company is active at the location where it began thirty-three years ago.

CINCINNATI PUBLISHERS

As far back as in the eighteen-forties Cincinnati had its music-publisher in the person of W. C. Peters, who carried on a branch house in Louisville, Ky. He was followed, in turn, by W. C. Peters & Sons, A. C. Peters & Bro., and Peters, Field & Co. A rival firm was conducted by J. L. Peters, followed by J. L. Peters & Bro. who had a branch house in St. Louis. This last-named firm was succeeded in the sixties by J. J. Dobmeyer & Co. who had their day until, together with Peters, Field & Co., they were absorbed by J. L. Peters of New York, who sold out to Oliver Ditson & Co. in 1877. Two other Cincinnati catalogs, those of F. W. Helmick and the Newhall & Evans Music Co., were also purchased by Oliver Ditson & Co., thus linking the Boston house to the beginnings of music-publishing in Cincinnati.

In 1849 a fourteen-year-old Rhode Island boy, John Church, entered the employ of Oliver Ditson of Boston, then at 115 Washington Street. In 1869, needing someone to straighten out a business tangle with the firm of Truax & Baldwin of Cincinnati, Mr. Ditson sent John Church, then twenty-five, who successfully accomplished his mission. Seeing the business possibilities of this rising city, Mr. Church negotiated with Mr. Ditson for a half-interest in the concern taken over, and thus on April 21, 1859, the firm of John Church, Jr., was started with Oliver Ditson as senior partner. On March 1, 1869, Mr. Church purchased the half-interest of Mr. Ditson and with John B. Trevor, his bookkeeper, changed the firm name to John Church & Co.

In October, 1871, the publication of Church's *Musical Visitor*, a monthly magazine, was begun and continued for twenty-six years. In 1873 the house purchased the catalog of George F. Root & Sons of Chicago who the year before had succeeded to the business of Root & Cady, established in 1858. This purchase added to their publications the famous warsongs of George F. Root and the popular song books: *Song King*, *Song Queen*, and others.

From 1862 to 1883 the house of Church specialized in popular stage songs, such as *Good Bye, Charlie; Not for Joseph; Whoa Emma!,* and *Baby Mine,* with others linked to the career of the comedian Sol. Smith Russell. They also issued the minstrel songs of J. K. Emmett, Billy Emerson, Gus Williams, Eddie Fox, and others, and at the same time the Moody & Sankey *Gospel Hymns* which had an unprecedented sale. In 1873 Church published a set of teaching pieces for the piano by the then unknown Theodore Presser.

Church's *Musical Visitor* for February, 1877, gives an account of the first meeting of the Music Teachers National Association, the call for which had been issued by Theodore Presser, then teaching at Wesleyan Female College, Delaware, Ohio. It was attended by such notables as George W. Chadwick, Lowell Mason, Eben Tourjée, George F. Root, and others.

From successful song-books for singing-schools and so-called "Musical Institutes" the firm in 1890 entered the professional operatic field, issuing many popular operettas by Sousa, Edwards, Hobart, de Koven, and others. Prior to this, and for some time after, the house published the popular marches of Sousa, Liberati, Innes, and other bandmasters. Later it was decided to publish the better-class music of the American composer as well as foreign copyrights, and the present policy of the house is along these lines.

Mr. John Church died in Boston, April 19, 1890.[*] Mr. R. B. Burchard, his son-in-law, became president

[*] Mr. Church's portrait is on page 71.

and Mr. W. L. Coghill was made general manager of the publication department, April 1, 1919. In April, 1930, the entire catalog was purchased by the Theodore Presser Company and the business moved to Philadelphia.

On April 1, 1899, Mr. Charles H. Willis, who for twenty-seven years had been with the John Church Company, started in business for himself at 41 East Fourth Street. In May, 1901, he purchased the miscellaneous stock of sheet-music and books of the John Church Company's retail business and moved to their store at Fourth and Elm Streets. Associated with Mr. Willis was his son William H., with the firm name W. H. Willis & Co. Beginning with the publication of teaching material, especially for piano-teachers, the publishing policy gradually broadened its scope on general lines. In 1910 the absorption of George B. Jennings & Co. led to the incorporation of the Willis Music Company. In 1911 the firm moved to its present location at 137 West Fourth Street, and later the growth of business led to the occupation of the entire seven-story building. On July 1, 1919, the control of the business passed into the hands of Mr. Gustave Schirmer of New York, son of the founder of the Boston Music Company and grandson of the founder of the house of G. Schirmer, Inc. This important Cincinnati house has made a specialty of teaching material together with school operettas, playlets, and cantatas, as well as octavo music, sacred and secular.

CHICAGO PUBLISHERS

While Chicago is for all commodities a great distributing center it has not yet become equally important as a publishing center. In the eighteen-sixties, or late fifties, H. M. Higgins and then Higgins Brothers published music at 117 Randolph Street, but this catalog was taken over by J. L. Peters of New York who, in turn, sold out to Oliver Ditson & Co. in 1877.

Chicago's pioneer publisher seems to have been Root & Cady (E. T. Root and C. M. Cady) established in 1858. The next year George F. Root of Massachusetts, brother of E. T. Root, became a partner. As organist, choralist, at one period a co-worker with Lowell Mason, and as a voice-teacher and composer, his association with the firm was invaluable. Upon the opening of the Civil War he began composing songs of enormous popularity, such as *The Battle-cry of Freedom*; *Just before the battle, mother*; *Tramp, tramp, tramp, the boys are marching*; *The vacant chair*, and many others. He also wrote cantatas of great popularity, among them *The Flower-Queen*; *Daniel* (1853); *The Pilgrim Fathers* (1854); *The Haymakers* (1857), and *Belshazzar's Feast* (1860). The great fire of 1871 changed the firm to George F. Root & Sons, who were absorbed in 1873 by John Church & Co. of Cincinnati, as already stated, while the cantatas named became part of the Oliver Ditson catalog.

Lyon & Healy published music for a while, then turned over this department of their business to Oliver

[132]

Ditson & Co. Music-publishing languished in Chicago until one man of courage, with a background of experience both as a music-teacher and as an employee of Lyon & Healy, felt that the time was ripe for a local publisher. Backed with stock supplied by the house of Schmidt, Schirmer, and Novello, Mr. Clayton F. Summy opened his establishment at 42 Madison Street on August 8, 1888. His slogan as dealer and publisher has been: "Music of the better class." Here again his experience as a teacher led Mr. Summy to work on educational lines, particularly in material for piano-teachers. During its forty-five years of business the Clayton F. Summy Company has occupied five different locations, each time moving south one block. For seventeen years the firm was located at 225 South Wabash Avenue. For the past thirteen years the Summy Company, with many of its original helpers, has been located at No. 429 South Wabash Avenue. On February 10, 1932, Mr. Summy died at his home in Hinsdale, Ill. This involved no change in the business which had been reorganized in the summer of 1931 with Mr. John F. Sengstack as president.

One Sunday evening in 1903 a music-lover and his wife were singing in church in the choir-loft the well-known duet, *Love Divine, all Love excelling*, from Sir John Stainer's cantata, *The Daughter of Jairus*, when, to their joint embarrassment, the unattached middle sheet of music dropped into the air but was recovered by a quick and undignified grab before it reached the floor.

This awkward incident set the man, William M. Gamble of Chicago, to thinking of some practical plan that would prevent its recurrence. After several years of experiment, Mr. Gamble perfected his unique plan and the necessary machinery for hinging printed music at a minimum cost. Having sought in vain to interest leading publishers and distributors of music in his invention, Mr. Gamble opened his own music-store in 1909 in the Wexford Building at the corner of Wabash Avenue and Van Buren Street. Six months later the Gamble Hinged Music Company moved to 64 East Van Buren Street, and in 1929 moved to their present location at 228 South Wabash Avenue. In their twenty-four years of music-publishing, all of it hinged, Mr. Gamble and his son Eugene E. Gamble have built up a general catalog of music and books especially designed to meet the present-day needs of music-teachers, choirmasters, and schools.

CONCLUSION

While this outline of the history of music-publishing in the United States, includes the chief names, many, less significant, are omitted; nor has anything been said of the publishers in Buffalo, Detroit, Dayton, Milwaukee, St. Louis, Louisville, Memphis, Vicksburg, New Orleans, Charleston, Washington, or San Francisco, for much of their output was sporadic and local rather than national. A complete history would require extended research and an elaborate volume.

Too little has been said of the individual publications of the old-time houses. As to the active publishers of today, the general character and trend of their output is known to all.

The history of music and the history of music-publishing in this country are inseparable, for one finds its reflection in the other. Fashions and modes in music come and go and publishers come and go with them, but the great art of *Music* lives on, and the enduring publisher is the one who keeps pace with its ceaseless advance and change — the unresting publisher with the forward look in his eyes and the love of music in his heart.

Common Street (now Tremont Street) Boston, in 1798
From the water-color by Archibald Robertson, the Scotch artist and the drawing-master of Washington Allston. It was once the property of John Howard Payne, the homeless author of *Home, Sweet Home*, who in his youth acted with success on the Boston stage.

INDEX

	Page		Page
Abt, Franz	69	Baltzell, W. J.	74
Academy of Music Orchestra	63	*Barber of Seville*	101
Adams and Liberty	37–39	Barnett, John	101
Adams and Washington	37	Battelle's Boston Book-store	15, 34
Adams, President	38	Battelle, Col. Ebenezer	34, 35, 84, 117
Ah! what is the bosom's commotion	97	*Battle Cry of Freedom*	132
Ainsworth, Henry	1	Baumbach, Adolph	60
Ainsworth Psalter	1	*Bay Psalm Book, The*	2, 3, 8
Aitken, John	26	Beach, Mrs. H. H. A.	119
Alboni, Marietta	66	Beacham, Joseph R.	95
Always take a mother's advice	111	Beacon Hill, Boston	xiv
American Guild of Organists	109	Beacon Street, Boston	xiv, xv
American Harmony, Holden	15	Beck, James M.	89
American Organ Quarterly	109	Beck & Lawton	89
Analytic Symphony Series	81	Beer, B.	103
André, G., & Co.	72, 75	Beer & Schirmer	103
Anona	113	Beethoven, L. van	13, 62
Antonene, Ship	104	Belder, George	105
Appel, John	101	Belknap, Daniel	58
Arabella, The Caledonian Maid	97	*Belshazzar's Feast*	132
Arne, Dr. Thomas A.	30, 56	Benteen & Co.	95
Arnold, Dr. Samuel	25, 26, 30	Benteen, Frederick D.	95
Ashton, John, & Company	115	Berlin, Irving, Inc.	113
Ashton, John, Jr.	115, 116	Berry, Thomas S.	98
Ashmall, William E.	126	Berry & Gordon	98
Astor, John Jacob	28	Billings, William	xv, 12–14, 58
Atwill, J. F.	74	Birchard, Clarence C.	127
Atwood, Thomas	30	Birchard, C. C. & Co.	127, 128
Autocrat of the Breakfast Table	xiii	Birch, Thomas	101
Austin, Henry R.	120	Bishop, Sir Henry	101
		Blackwell, Henry B.	61
Baby Mine	130	Blagrove, William	39, 40, 84, 117
Bach, John Sebastian	8, 57, 69	Blake, George E.	26, 87
Bacon, Allyn	87	Blake, William Pinson	35
Bacon & Co.	88	Blanchard, L. W.	74
Bacon & Hart	88	Blaxton, Rev. William	xiv, xv
Bacon, Weygand & Co.	88	*Blind King, The*, Parker	57
Baltimore	xvi	*Blossom Time*	113
Baltimore Publishers	27, 28, 93–95	Boner, W. H., & Co.	89

[137]

	Page
Boosey & Co., Ltd.	109
Boston Book-store	34, 35
Boston Common	xiii–xvi
Boston Magazine	31
Boston Music Company	122–124, 131
Boston Publishers	
36, 37, 40–46, 50–62, 71–82	
Boyce, William	21
Bradbury, William B.	59
Bradford, Gov. William	53
Bradlee, Charles	42, 43, 74, 116
Braham, John	86
Brattle Organ	9, 10
Brattle Square Church	4, 9
Brattle, Thomas	9, 10
Brignoli, Pasqualino	66
Bristow, George F.	57
Brett, Arabella	30
Broadhurst, Miss	30
Brooks, Rev. Phillips	76
Brentano Bros.	74
Breusing, Charles	103
Brown, William	19
Buck, Dudley	57, 60, 68, 70, 102
Bull, Ole	47, 67, 68
Bülow, Hans von	67
Bunker Hill	xiv–xv
Burchard, R. B.	130
Burnet, Gov. William	10
Caecilia, The	127
Cady, C. M.	132
Calcott, Dr. John W.	56
Calvé, Emma	80
Cambridge	xiv, xv, 2
Cambridge Short Tune	3
Capron, Henry	25
Carr, B., & Co.	25, 26
Carr, Benjamin	25, 27, 29, 30, 86
Carr, Joseph	27, 29, 93, 94
Carr & Schetky	25, 86
Carr, Thomas	28, 93, 94
Carreño, Teresa	67
Catholic Music Publishing Co.	127
Centennial Exposition	70

	Page
Century Edition	113
Charleston, S. C.	10
Chadwick, George W.	119, 130
Chicago Publishers	xvi, 71
Choirs	12
Chopin, Frederic	47
Christ Church, Boston	11
Christ Church, Cambridge	xv
Christ Church, Baltimore	93
Christmas Oratorio, Bach	57
Christy, Edward T.	100
Christy Minstrels	110
Chronology of Oliver Ditson Company	84, 85
Church, John	71, 85, 93, 129, 130
Church, John, Jr.	129
Church, John, Co.	71, 79, 130, 131
Church, John, & Co.	129, 132
Church Music Review	109
Cincinnati Publishers	xvi, 71, 75
City Guards Quick-step	51
Clarke, Dr. John	56
Coghill, W. L.	131
Cole, George T.	95
Cole, John	94
Cole, John, & Son	95
Collection of the Best Psalm Tunes, Flagg	11, 58
Columbian Songster, The	15
Concert Etude, Whiting	122
Concert Hall, Boston	17
Concerts of Music	16–19
Contented Cottager, The	97
Continental Harmony, Billings	14
Cooke, Benjamin	101
Cooke, James Francis	93
Copley, John Singleton	36
Copley, Mary	36
Coronation, Holden	15
Cortada, A., & Co.	74
Cranch, Christopher P.	65
Crazy Jane	97
Creation, The, Haydn	57, 86
Crosby, Harry B.	120
Culp, Julia	81

[138]

Damrosch, Dr. Leopold	57	Eden Musée	110
Danks, H. P.	103	*Edition Wood*	125
Daniel, Root	132	Edwards, Julian	130
Darley, H. W.	59	Eichberg, Julius	61, 68
David, Neukomm	52	*Elijah*, Mendelssohn	57
Deblois, Gilbert	17	Emerson, Billy	130
Delano, Catherine	53	Emerson, L. O.	59, 61
Der Freischütz, Weber	101	Emerson, Ralph Waldo	xiv, 47
Dibdin, Charles	21, 26, 30	Emery, Florence J.	120
Dickinson, John	21	Emmett, J. K.	130
Dickson, James A.	43	Essipoff, Annette	67
Ditson Buildings		*Etude, The*	90, 91, 93
55, 56, 72, 73, 77, 78, 84, 85, 100			
Ditson Catalogs	75, 76, 79	Falckner, Justus	10
Ditson, Charles H.		Faneuil Hall	17
71, 76–80, 85, 93, 99, 100		Faneuil, Peter	17
Ditson, Chas. H., & Co.		Farrar, Geraldine	81
71, 78, 85, 99, 100		Father Streeter's Church	9
Ditson, James Edward	72, 85	Fay, W. Rodman	104
Ditson, J. E., & Co.	72, 85, 87	*Festival Cantata*, Thayer	57
Ditson, Joseph	46, 47	Fields, James T.	53
Ditson, Oliver	xiv, 43, 46–53	Fiot, Augustus	75, 88, 89
55–57, 69, 76, 79, 84, 85, 93		Fiot, Meignen & Co.	88
Ditson, Oliver, & Co.		Fischer, Carl	105, 106
26, 56, 59, 60, 65, 71, 73, 77		Fischer, George	107
85, 87–89, 95, 99, 116–118		Fischer, J., & Bro.	107
120, 121, 128, 129, 132, 133		Fischer, Joseph	107
Ditson, Oliver, Company		Fischer, Walter S.	107
76, 78, 79, 85, 93, 100		First Music-publishers	23–31
Ditson, Oliver, Company,		First Music-shops	23–31
Chronology of	84, 85	First Music-teachers	20, 45
Ditson, Samuel	46	First Music-type	15
Dobson, Thomas	24	First Song Published	20
Does true love ever run		Firth & Hall	98, 99
smooth?	113	Firth, Hall & Pond	99
Dreyschock, Alexander	57	Firth, John	98, 99
Dubois, William	98	Firth, Pond & Co.	99, 100
Dubois & Bacon	98	Firth, Son & Co.	71, 72, 74, 99
Dubois & Stodart	98	Firth, Thaddeus	99
Dubois & Warriner	98	*Five chiefs of renown*	97
Dutch Psalter	1	Flammer, Harold	105
Dutch Reformed Church	1	Flammer, Harold, Inc.	105
Dwight, John S.	54, 57, 65, 68	*For then I had not learned of love*	96
Dwight's Journal of Music		Foster, Stephen	100
65, 66, 68, 73, 85		Fuller, Margaret	54

	Page		Page
Gambler's Wife, The	101	Grisi, Giulia	66
Gamble Hinged Music Company	134	Grounds and Rules of Musick	7
Gamble, Eugene E.	134	Guild, Benjamin	35, 42, 84
Gamble, William M.	134	Gunther, Edwin L.	108
Garcia, Manuel	101	Gunther, Emil A.	108
Garrison, William Lloyd	47		
Gehrkens, Karl	81	Hail! Columbia	26, 37, 38
Gerhardt, Elena	81	Hale, Philip	73
Gericke, Wilhelm	65	Hall, William	98, 99
Germania Orchestra	63	Hall, William, & Son	72, 74, 99
Geib, Adam	97	Hamilton, Clarence	81
Geib, John	97	Handel and Haydn Society	
Geib, John and Adam, & Co.	97		40, 48, 49, 51, 62, 64, 69
Geib, John, & Co.	97	Handel and Haydn Society	
Geib & Walker	97	Collection	48
Geib, William	97	Handel, George F.	8, 12, 18, 21, 57
Gilfert, George	28, 95–97	Haney, H. J.	vii
Gilmore, Patrick S.	68, 69, 118	Harms, T. B., Inc.	113
Gloria Dei Church, Philadelphia	10	Harrigan and Hart	110
Gluck, Alma	81	Harrison, James	29
Gluck, C. W. von	21	Harvard Musical Association	64, 65
Goetschius, Percy	81	Hastings, Thomas	59
Goldschmidt, Otto	66	Hawthorne, Alice	89
Good Bye, Charlie	130	Hawthorne, Nathaniel	47
Gordon, Hamilton A.	102	Haydn, Josef	21, 26, 29, 46, 57
Gordon, Hamilton S.	102	Haymakers, Root	132
Gordon, Herbert	102	Haynes, John C.	55, 76, 77, 80, 85
Gordon, Leslie	102	Healy, P. J.	71
Gordon, Stephen T.	97–99, 102	Hearts of Oak, Boyce	21
Gordon, S. T., & Co.	102	Helmick, F. W.	75, 129
Gordon, S. T., & Son	102	Henschel, George	65
Gospel Hymns	130	Hewitt & Jaques	96
Gottschalk, Louis M.	67	Hewitt, James	29, 96
Gould, John E.	89	Hewitt, James L.	30, 97, 116
Gould, J. E., & Co.	88, 98	Hewitt, James L., & Co.	96
Gould & Berry	98, 102	Higgins Brothers	132
Graupner, Gottlieb		Higgins, H. M.	132
vii, 38, 40, 41, 45, 46, 48, 49, 56, 114		Higginson, Henry Lee	64
Graupner & Mallet	115	Higginson, Thomas Wentworth	62
Graupner, John Henry H.	49, 56	Hillegas, Michael	23
Graupner, Mrs. Catherine	38, 46	Hodgkinson, John	30, 38
Gray, H. W., Co.	109	Holden, Oliver	14, 15, 58
Gray, H. Willard	108	Hollis Street Tune	13
Gray, Matthias	75	Holmes, Oliver Wendell	47
Greatorex, Henry W.	59	Holyoke, Samuel	58

	Page
Home for Retired Music Teachers	92
Hook, James	21, 26, 30
Hopkinson, Francis	24, 27
Horn, Charles E.	101
Howe, Julia Ward	61
Hymn of Praise, Mendelssohn	57
I*'d be a butterfly*	101
I'll answer that question tomorrow	111
I'm goin' back to Dixie	121
Independent Musical Society	18
Innes, F. N.	130
Irene	113
Irion, Hermann	104
Jackson, Dr. William	26
Jamestown, Va.	1
Jaques, Edward I.	101
Jaques, James M.	101
Jaques, John D.	101
Jennings, George B., & Co.	131
Jennings, Joseph M.	vii
Joshua, Handel	57
Judas Maccabeus, Handel	57
Just before the battle, mother	132
Keith, Charles H.	74, 115
Keith & Moore	115
Kempf, Paul	74
Kelley, Edgar Stillman	81
Kelley, Michael	30, 97
Kerksieg & Breusing	103
Kerksieg, Evich	103
Kimball, Jacob	58
King's Chapel, Boston	47, 48
Klemm, Johann G.	11
Klemm, J. G., & Bro.	88
Knoefel, H.	75
Knox, Henry	34, 41
Koek, Hendrick M.	10
Koppitz, Charles	120
Koppitz, Prüffer & Co.	120
Kranz, G. Fred, Music Company	94

	Page
Lane, Frederick	115
Lang, B. J.	68
Laurel Song Book	127
Law, Andrew	58
Lawton, Dennis	89
Lawton, J. W., & Co.	89
Lee, Alexander	101
Lee, George W.	87
Lee & Walker	26, 72, 75, 87
Leipzig Conservatory	90
Liberati, A.	130
Liberty Song	20, 36
Lind, Jenny	66
Lining out the Psalms	4
Linley, Thomas	30
Listen to the Mocking Bird	89
Liszt, Franz	47
Liturgical Music Company	127
Livermore, Mary A.	62
London Book-store	33, 34, 36
Longfellow, Henry W.	47
Love Divine, all Love excelling	133
Lovely Jane	97
Lover, Samuel	101
Lyon & Healy	71, 85, 132, 133
Lyon, George W.	71
Lyon, Rev. James	12
Luckhardt & Belder	105
Luckhardt, George C.	105
MacDowell, Edward	70, 119, 120
Malibran, Maria	101
Mallet, Francis	115
Maniac, The, Russell	101
Marguerite, White	121
Mario, Giuseppi	66
Marks, E. B., Music Company	113
Mark the busy insect playing	97
Marriage of Figaro, Mozart	101
Marseillaise, The	xiv
Martens Bros.	74
Mason Brothers	74
Mason, Daniel Gregory	81
Mason, Lowell	48, 49, 59–61, 102, 127, 130, 132

	Page		Page
Mason, William	57, 63	*Musical Asylum*, Philadelphia	31
Massachusetts Magazine	31	Musical Fund Society, Phila.	63, 86
Mather, Dr. Cotton	8, 9	*Musical Observer, The*	106
Mayell, John	100	*Musical Quarterly, The*	105
Mayflower Pilgrims	1	*Musical Record, The*	73
Maxwell, George	109	*Musical Record and Review*	73
Mazzinghi, Joseph	56	*Musical Visitor*, Church's	129
McCaffrey, Henry C.	75, 95	*Musician, The*	74
McLaughlin, James M.	126	*Musicians Library*	80
McLaughlin & Reilly	126	*My Country, 'tis of Thee*	xv
Meacham & Pond	99		
Medfield Tune	13	Narcissus, Nevin	122
Mehlig, Anna	67	Negro Minstrelsy	110
Meignen, Leopold	88	Nevin, Ethelbert	122
Mein, John	33	New Amsterdam	1
Mendelssohn, Felix	57	New England Conservatory	
Mendelssohn Quintette Club	65	of Music	90, 124
Messiah, The, Handel		*New England Psalm Singer*	12
	12, 48, 52, 57, 86	Newhall & Evans Music Co.	75, 129
Metcalf, Frank J.	vii	*New Method*, Richardson	58
Metronome, The	106	*New Music Review and Church*	
Michaelis, Gustav	106	*Music Review*	109
Miles & Thompson	119	New York	xvi
Miller & Beacham	75, 95	*New York Magazine*	31
Miller, William C.	95	New York Publishers	28-31, 95-114
Millet, William E.	101	Nikisch, Arthur	65
Millard, Harrison	103	North, Francis A.	88
Mitchell's Class Methods	80	North, F. A., & Co.	73, 75, 88
Modern School, Richardson	58	Note Singing, Innovation of	6
Moller & Capron	24	*Notes on Music in Old Boston*	xvi
Moller, John C	25, 26	*Not for Joseph*	130
Monthly Musical Record	73	Novello, Ewer & Co.	108, 109, 133
Morgan, George W.	68		
Mornington, Earl of	56	Oakes, W. H.	117
Mozart, W. A.	12, 21, 26, 56, 101	*Ode from Ossian's Poems*	27
Munroe, Francis & Parker	40	Old Corner Bookstore	53, 55
Music Hall, Boston	63	*Old Folks at Home*	100
Music in Miniature, Billings	14	Oldmixon, Mrs.	30
Musical Journal	86	Old St. Paul's Church, Baltimore	93
Music Review	73	Oliver, Henry K.	65
Music Students Library	80	*One Spring Morning*, Nevin	122
Music Students Piano Course	81	*Oratorio of David*, Neukomm	52
Music Study in Public Schools	60	Ordway, A. & J. P.	74, 117
Music Teachers National		Organs, Use of	xv, 9-11, 15
Association	90, 130	Organ, Great Music Hall	58, 67

[142]

	Page		Page
Organ Pedals	11	*Plain and Easy Introduction*	6
Organist's Journal, The	126	Pleyel, Ignaz	21, 29, 86
Over there	113	Plymouth Colony	1
Oxford University Press	107	*Pocket Music Student, The*	82
		Poet and Peasant, overture	106
PACHELBEL, Mr.	19	Pond, G. Warren	101
Paff, John	30, 95	Pond, Sylvanus B.	99
Paff, John and M.	30	Pond, William A.	99–101
Paine, John K.	57, 68, 70, 119	Popular Publishers	110–114
Paine, Robert Treat	38	Porter, H. Hobart	79, 85
Palma, John	19	Pownall, Mrs.	30
Park Street Church, Boston	xv, 9	*Praise to God*, George F. Bristow	57
Parker & Ditson 52, 55, 56, 84, 85, 117		Prentiss, Henry	115
		Presser Company, Theodore 79, 85, 90–93, 100, 131	
Parker, Col. Samuel Hale 39–44, 48–50, 56, 84, 116		Presser Foundation	92, 93
Parker, J. C. D.	57, 76	Presser, Theodore	130
Patti, Adelina	66	Preston, John Aiken	125
Peace Jubilee of 1869	68	Preston, W. Deane, Jr.	126
Peace Jubilee of 1872	62, 69	Priaulx, J. M.	vii
Peg o' my heart	113	Price, William	36
Pelham, Peter	36	Prüffer, Carl	74, 120
Pelham, Sarah	39	*Psalm 46*, Buck	57
Pelham, William	35, 36, 39, 84	*Psalm Singer's Amusement*	14
Perkins, H. L.	61	Public School Music	60, 61
Perkins, W. O.	59, 61	Pucitta, Vincenzo	97
Perry, John F.	121	Puritan Congregation	12
Perry, J. F., & Co.	74	Puritanism	5
Peters, A. C., & Bro.	128		
Peters, Field & Co.	128	QUEEN'S Chapel, Boston	9
Peters, J. L.	72, 74, 99, 128, 132		
Peters, J. L., & Bro.	128	R*amona*	113
Peters, William C.	101, 128	Ravenscroft, Thomas	2
Peters, W. C., & Sons	128	Read, Charles F.	vii
Petsworth Church, Va.	11	Read, Daniel	58
Philadelphia	xvi	*Redemption Hymn*, Parker	57
Philadelphia Publishers	23–26, 86–93	Reed, George P.	117
Philharmonic Orchestra, Boston	64	Reed, George P., & Co.	117
Philharmonic Orchestra Series	81	Reeve, William	30
Philharmonic Society, Boston	46	Riley & Adams	98
Phillips, Adelaide	66, 68	Riley, Edward	96–98
Phillips, Wendell	xiv	Riley, Edward C.	98
Picture that's turned to the wall	111	Riley, Elizabeth	98
Pilgrim Fathers, Root	132	Riley, Frederick	98
Pitch-pipe	14	Reilly, Dr. James A.	126

Reinagle, Alexander	24
Remenyi, Eduard	67
Remick Music Corporation	113
Revere, Paul	11
Rink's Organ School	58
Richardson, Nathan	57, 58, 117
Ricordi, G., & Co.	109, 110
Rio Rita	113
Rivington, James	33
Rivington & Miller	33
Robbins Music Corporation	113
Robinson, Harold W.	126
Root & Cady	129, 132
Root, E. T.	132
Root, George F.	59, 60, 129, 130, 132
Root, George F., & Sons	129, 132
Rosa, Carl	68
Rosa, Parepa	66, 68
Rossini, Giacomo	57, 101
Rottenbach, A.	75
Rubinstein, Anton	67
Rudersdorff, Hermine	69
Russell Bros.	74, 118
Russell, George D.	73, 117
Russell, G. D., & Co.	74, 118
Russell & Fuller	117
Russell, Henry	54, 101
Russell, Joseph M.	117, 118
Russell & Patee	118
Russell & Richardson	117
Russell & Tolman	117
Russell, Sol. Smith	130
Ruth and Naomi, Damrosch	57
Ryan, Thomas	9, 65
S<small>ALTER</small>, John	10, 19
Samson, Handel	57
Sauret, Émile	67
Scharfenberg & Luis	103
Schirmer, E. C., Music Company	124
Schirmer, Edward	124
Schirmer, Ernest C.	124
Schirmer, G., Inc.	104, 105, 131, 133
Schirmer, Gustav	103, 122–124
Schirmer, Gustave, Jr.	104, 122–124
Schirmer, Gustave, 3d	104, 123, 131
Schirmer, Rudolph E.	104, 122, 123
Schmidt, Arthur Paul	118–120, 125
Schmidt, Arthur P., Company	120
Schroeder, John Ferdinand	108
Schroeder, John Henry	108
Schroeder & Gunther, Inc.	108
Schumann, Robert	47
Secular Music-publishing	21
Selby, William	18
Sembrich, Marcella	81
Semi-popular Songs	111
Sengstack, John F.	133
Seven Songs for the Harpsichord, Hopkinson	24
Sewall, Judge Samuel	7
Shapiro, Bernstein & Co., Inc.	113
Shaw & Co.	26
Shaw, Oliver	41, 58
Shaw, Ralph	86
Shaw, Robert	26
Shaw, W. F.	75
Shield, William	21, 26, 30, 56, 86, 97
Ship on Fire, The	101
Silver, Burdett & Co.	127
Silver threads among the gold	102
Singenberger, John B.	127
Singing Master's Assistant	13
Singing Schools established	7
Sivori, Camillo	67
Sketch Book, Nevin	122
Smith, John Stafford	38
Smith, W. Frank	121
Smoky Mokes	113
Soldier tired, The	97
Song King, The, Root	129
Song Queen, The, Root	129
Sontag, Henrietta	66
Sonneck, Oscar G.	vii, 31, 104, 105
Sousa, John Philip	130
Spear & Denhoff	74
Sprögell, Ludovic	10
Stabat Mater, Rossini	57
Stainer, Sir John	133
Stanbridge, J. C. B.	59

Standard Publishers	112
Star Spangled Banner	27, 39
St. Coecilia Society	19
Stevenson, Sir John	56
Strike the Cymbal, Puccita	97
St. Matthew Passion, Bach	57, 69
Stone Chapel, Boston	18
Stone, Lucy	61
Stone, Mrs. George Whitefield	vii
Story, William Wetmore	65
Stoughton Musical Society	14
St. Peter, John K. Paine	57
St. Philip's Church, Charleston	10
Storace, Stephen	21, 26, 30
Storer, Maria	30
Stowe, Harriet Beecher	47
Strauss, Johann	69
Study Course in Music Understanding	81
Sumner, Charles	47
Suppé, Franz von	106
Surette, Thomas Whitney	124
Summy, Clayton F.	133
Summy, Clayton F., Company	133
Swan, Timothy	58
Symphonic Band Series	81
Tate & Brady's Version	8
Tansur's Royal Melody	33
Tasselli, Dr. Renato	109
Taylor, Raynor	25
Thackeray, William M.	47
Thatcher, Primrose & West	110
Thayer, Eugene	57, 68
Thayer, Mary Alden	vii
There's not a leaf within the bower	50
Thomas, Isaiah	15
Thompson, C. W., & Co.	119
Three o'clock in the morning	113
Tin-Pan-Alley	113, 114
To Arms, Columbia	37
Tolman, Henry	117
Tolman, Henry, & Co.	117
Tourjée, Eben	130
Tramp, tramp, tramp, the boys are marching	132
Trevor, John B.	129
Trinity Church, Boston	11, 76
Trinity Church, Newport	9–11
Trinity Church, New York	11
Truax & Baldwin	129
Trumpler, Charles W. A.	88
Tuckerman, S. P.	68
Turkish Patrol	106
Tuttle, Julius H.	vii
Under the daisies	103
Urania, Lyon	12
Urso, Camilla	67
Vacant Chair, The	132
Vaudeville	110
Vieuxtemps, Henri	67
Violoncello, introduced in churches	14
Von Hagen, Peter Albrecht	28, 36, 37, 114, 115
Von Hagen, P. A., & Co.	37
Wade, E. H.	74, 115, 116
Wahle, J. H., & Son	75
Walker, Julius	87
Walker, William W.	87
Walter, Rev. Thomas	7
Warner Brothers	112
Warville, Brissot de	20
Washington, General	xv, 47
Water Scenes, Nevin	122
Waters, Horace	101
Watkins, Walter Kendall	vii
Webb, George J.	59, 61
Webbe, Dr. Samuel	56
Weber, C. M. von	101
What is Home without a Mother?	89
When the leaves begin to turn	121
Whispering Hope, Winner	89
White, Charles A.	120, 121
White, Daniel L.	121
White-Smith Music Company	121

	Page		Page
White-Smith & Co.	121	Winner, J. Gibson	89
White-Smith & Perry	121	Winner, Joseph	89
Whiting, Arthur	122	Winner & Schuster	89
Whittier, John G.	47	Winner, Septimus	75, 89
Whoa! Emma	130	Winner, Septimus & Son	89
Wieniawski, Henri	67	Witmark, Isidore	111
Wignell, Thomas	30	Witmark, M., & Sons	111, 112
Wilcox, John H.	68	Witmark, Julius P.	110–112
Wilhelmj, August	67	Woodbridge, William C.	49
Williams, Gus	130	Woodbury, Isaac B.	59
Willig, George	26, 86, 87, 94	Woodward, Willis, Company	111
Willig, George, Jr.	94	Wood, B. F.	124–126
Willig, George, & Co.	94	Wood, B. F., Music Co.	124–126
Willig, Henry	94	*Worcester Collection*, Holden	15
Willig, Joseph E.	94		
Willis, Charles H.	131	Yankee Doodle	xiv
Willis, William H.	131	*York Tune*	3, 7
Willis, W. H., & Co.	131		
Willson, Joseph	101	Zerrahn, Carl	64, 68
Windsor Tune	3, 7	Zeuner, Charles	51, 59